not
by
accident

not
by
accident

not by accident

Cloé Madanes

A Memoir

Zeig, Tucker & Theisen, Publishers
Phoenix, Arizona

Copyright 2022 Cloé Madanes

Published by
Zeig, Tucker & Theisen, Inc.
Phoenix, AZ 85016
www.zeigtucker.com

To my students.

PSYCHOTHERAPY HAS EVOLVED IN context, not within the limiting confines of personality structure. And the experts who advance psychotherapy are influenced by their developmental history, historical context, and familial forces.

Cloé Madanes has been an extraordinary force in evolving psychotherapy. Her work has immeasurably built both practice and theory. In *Not by Accident*, we are privileged to learn about the influences that have shaped her inventive approach and remarkable life.

Written without the handicapping constraints of convention, this is a no-holds-barred description of the professional life of one of history's most inventive and humanistic therapists. We learn about developmental and cultural forces that mold therapists. We learn about the effect of relationships with luminaries including Milton Erickson, Jay Haley, R.D. Laing, Salvador Minuchin, and Virginia Satir. Tony Robbins makes a center stage entrance.

Peppered throughout the engrossing narrative are techniques that will improve the practice of therapists—whether beginners or experts. And these valuable methods are placed in the context from which they evolved.

This is an intriguing story of meeting adversity with unfaltering courage. It is the story of how privilege so often walks side by side with hardship. It is the story of one woman's overwhelming success within an ecology of tenacious misogyny. It is a simply told story that highlights the complexity of lineage, relationship, and contribution.

What essential do we learn from Cloé? Creativity is breath. Good humor is bedrock. And forgiveness is more than a bumper sticker; it is the difference between resentment and resilience. Cloé dropped breadcrumbs from a very early age, hints of where she would find meaning. In *Not by Accident*, she retraces them to show us where meaning has found her.

Jeffrey K. Zeig, PhD
Director
The Milton H. Erickson Foundation

CONTENTS

The Accomplice

I belong to the generation born into psychotherapy during the great years of psychoanalysis. Between the Second World War and the Vietnam War, there was the feeling that therapists were going to discover the essence of human nature. The dark side of mankind would be understood and controlled; atrocities would not be repeated. My interest in psychotherapy, from a very young age, was generated in the idealism of those times.

I wanted to figure out how to change people and how to change them in fundamental ways. In order to understand the stigmatized, the sordid, the perverse, the ugly, a therapist must, to some extent, become an accomplice in the experiences of evil and pathos. To bring someone out of deep pain, one must experience the grief that the other feels. In a family, there is always the victim and the victimizer, the good and the evil, the joyful and the pathetic. As a therapist I have been an accomplice to all.

My purpose in writing this memoir is to capture the incongruities and contradictions in my life and relate them to how I developed the flexibility and tolerance necessary to understand how love and violence can coexist, how we use each other to survive, how we protect those we love at the same time that we hurt them and are hurt by them, how everything in the human condition is paradoxical.

As is the case with most people, my life was inextricably intertwined with the socio-political context in which I lived. I want to show how the political situations that I navigated affected my relationships, influenced my interests and my thinking, and led to the therapy strategies that I developed, which, in turn, influenced my relationships. The memoir can be seen as a tapestry composed of many different threads. Something happened politically … my family was affected … I had to make sense of what was happening … my focus and the meaning I gave to events changed … I transformed these experiences into strategies to intervene in people's lives in positive ways. This transformation might have happened many years later, but it originated in the social context of my past.

By telling my story I want to show how experiences that could be viewed as negative have inspired my most creative work as a psychotherapist. I tell my story in terms of bridges between my experiences, my thoughts, my emotions, my work, and the things that were happening in the world around me at any given time.

CHAPTER 1

Revolution

There was a noise outside the window that sounded like the intermittent backfiring of cars. I felt too sick to get out of bed to see what was going on.

My father came into the room and asked how I was feeling.

I told him, "I'm better, but there are strange noises coming from outside."

He pulled back the heavy brocade curtain and looked out onto the street. "I have to go," he said.

I didn't know that bombs were falling on the city, but at that moment I had the sinking feeling that my life was changing for the worse.

My father left for his office where he worked as the director of the national television station.

I later heard my mother on the phone pleading with him to come home. She explained to me that the military were bombing the city in an attempt to oust Juan Perón. She feared for my father's life.

The coup had failed, and it would be three more months before Perón was ousted, marking the beginning of a military dictatorship that would last for years and during which many of my relatives and friends would be tortured and killed. For now, I was safe in the luxury of the palace where we lived.

My parents had rented the second floor of a building known as Palacio Devoto, an enormous residence belonging to the Devoto family who lived on the other four floors. My mother had lavishly decorated the apartment. While on a trip to Paris with my father, she had purchased furniture, fabrics, and antiques and had everything shipped to Buenos Aires. The floor of the huge circular entrance was white marble and the only object in the room was an 18th-century sculpture of a young naked woman. Then came the gallery where the walls were decorated with relief sculptures in 19th-century style. The living room was Louis XIV, with real gold leaf on the walls, and my father's study was done in French 18-century style and included boiserie paneling. It's hard to understand why they would spend all this money on decorating and remodeling a rented apartment, or why they would rent instead of buying. I imagine they were buying into the prestige of living in the mansion of one of the oldest aristocratic families of Argentina, who had streets and even a neighborhood named after them. I reveled in French existentialist literature and thought this decor was a crass display of nouveau riche bourgeoisie tastes. The contradiction that puzzled me was that my mother didn't care at all about the Argentine aristocracy, or any aristocracy, and what my father really cared about was education, equal opportunity, democracy, music, and poetry, among other higher pursuits.

On that day in 1955, June 16, 850 civilians, many of them children, were killed. The coup failed because not all branches of the military had joined the revolt. Perón, a populist president, had the support of the General Confederation of Labor but was criticized for his treatment of dissidents and lost the support of the Catholic church. My father was not a Peronist, but he had done business with men who were close to Perón, in particular a business deal involving importing television sets from the United

States. The television station where my father was the director was the only one in Argentina at the time. Only two shows were on late at night: the news and a once-a-week cabaret style musical series. I remember many instances of my father angrily screaming on the phone, "Cut to a commercial! Cut to a Commercial! I said no kissing and no touching!" We lived in a Catholic country.

My father was also involved in a negotiation to purchase the Polish Bank of Buenos Aires. His partner, Jorge Antonio, an Argentine of Arab descent, was the representative of Mercedes Benz in Argentina and a friend and advisor to Perón. He was very wealthy. I remember visiting his ranch where he raised horses for racing. I think the Polish bank was dear to my father's heart because his father was Polish and had run away from Poland at the age of 16. Almost all the members of his family were murdered by the Nazis, so the Polish Bank had a symbolic meaning for him. Ironically, many years later, I found out that Jorge Antonio, a shady character to say the least, had employed the infamous Nazi, Adolf Eichmann, at Mercedes Benz in Buenos Aires. He did so with full knowledge of who Eichmann was.

I would be turning 15 years old on August 14, 1955, and I had been promised a trip to Europe for my birthday. As the date approached, I insisted, "You promised me, you promised me. When are we going?"

*　*　*

At long last the date was set. We were leaving for Madrid on September 9. We would be gone for a month. In the beginning of September, I became quite sick. I had boils on different parts of my body. I knew I had a fever but didn't tell anyone because I feared the trip would be cancelled. I managed to keep my condition hidden from the nanny and from my mother.

We boarded the plane for the 24-hour flight to Madrid, stopping in Rio and in Dakar. I sat next to my father who, a few hours into the trip, remarked, "You don't look well. You seem feverish.

Have some champagne. It'll help you feel better." In those days in Argentina, teenagers were frequently offered wine or champagne.

When we were finally settled at the Ritz in Madrid, I announced, "I'm very sick. I need a doctor." I lay in bed in the hotel for a week with a fever. On September 16, the military once again bombed the city of Buenos Aires, that time succeeding in ousting Perón and ending his second presidential term. If we had stayed in Argentina, my father would have been killed, or at least imprisoned, maybe tortured. We later heard that Jorge Antonio had been arrested and sent to a prison in a remote southern region of the country. He would remain there for more than two years until he eventually escaped. His properties were seized and stolen. The Polish Bank was gone, and apparently my father had signed some kind of power of attorney to Jorge Antonio after investing 5 million dollars that was now also gone.

When I recovered, we flew to Paris because it was easier to communicate with Buenos Aires from there. It was no Ritz, just a modest hotel. I realized that from one day to the next I had fallen in social class. Not only that, but now we were in exile. We couldn't return to Argentina, and we had reason to fear for our lives. When I say we, I mean my mother, father, me, and my younger sister and brother (although my siblings were oblivious to the situation).

Lieutenant General Lonardi served as de facto president until November 13, 1955, when an internal coup deposed him and placed General Aramburu, a hard-liner anti Peronist in the presidency. Aramburu immediately jailed 9,000 union leaders and enacted restrictions, such as the ban on mentioning Perón's name. We were still in Europe.

*　*　*

When I was 9 years old, my Polish grandfather died of a heart attack. He had gone to Poland in 1946 in search of his family and found only two survivors. He came back to Buenos Aires with a broken heart. When he died, my father was inconsolable. It was the only time I saw him cry. My mother didn't know how to help him, and she began to rely on me. "Go talk to your father. Cuddle up with him. You always help him to feel better." And I did. I think that was when I first discovered my therapeutic powers and my vocation. What could be more gratifying to a little girl than to be able to help her young handsome father? I think that was the first time I thought that I needed to take care of my father, that I had to protect him. Many years later, in my first book, *Strategic Family Therapy*, I would write about children's need to protect and take care of their parents, and how sometimes they do so at the cost of their own well-being.

In *Strategic Family Therapy*, I discussed some of the reasons for a child's disturbed behavior, and offered:

"A parent might have trouble at work, difficulties with relatives, or his spouse might be threatening separation, but the parents will set aside their own problems, at least temporarily, to help or to control their child. They will try to overcome their own deficiencies and hold themselves together in order to aid the child. In this sense, the child's disturbed behavior is helpful to his parents. It provides a respite from the parents' own troubles and a reason to overcome their own difficulties. Whether the child's behavior provokes helpful, protective, or punitive acts from the parents, it focuses the parents' concern on him and makes the parents see themselves as parents to a child who needs them rather than as individuals overwhelmed by personal, economic, or social difficulties. In this sense, the child is a concerned benefactor or protector of others in his family."

Actually, as a child, it never occurred to me to act in disturbing ways to call attention to myself in order to distract my parents from their own problems. I didn't have to. My mother had asked me directly for help with my father and my father had directly expressed gratitude for my love and concern. I am grateful for my parents' courage to express their vulnerability and to allow me to help in straightforward ways. Many of the problems that children face could be avoided if parents would express their own vulnerability and allow their child to help. But today, this would go against what is considered good childrearing practices, so I developed many therapy strategies to allow children to be protective in indirect ways. For example, one of my "pretending" techniques is to ask a parent to pretend to be afraid and to allow the child to reassure and protect the parent. This gives the child the opportunity to be protective, even though the parent is just "pretending" and the interaction is make-believe.

Another strategy I created that has with roots in my childhood is "reversing the hierarchy." It applies to families where the parents are unhappy, incompetent, or quarreling with each other. The children are asked to give advice to the parents on how to be happy and how to get along. I have used it with children of all ages, including young adults. As the children advise the parents, the parents are moved by how well the children understand them and how much they care, and typically the parents respond by becoming more competent and kinder towards each other.

When my grandfather died, I also went through a period of grief. He was a very kind and loving man. In the summers, he would come to visit us at our beach house where he shared a room with me. He wore a nightgown and a hat. Before going to sleep, he listened to classical music on the Victrola that was kept in the bedroom. I loved him. My mother, who grew up in poverty, didn't believe that children should have toys. My grandfather would send us boxes full of toys on the Day of the Three Kings.

I desperately wanted to keep my grandfather alive. I remember that I deliberately decided that if I looked and behaved like my grandfather, he would be alive in me. I began to pace the floor, holding my hands behind my back, like he used to do. I imitated his smile and people began to comment about how much I resembled him. I decided I would be generous to a fault like he was. Years later I discovered that Freud described this process as "Introjection," the mechanism of defense by which a person incorporates the characteristics of another, usually because of grief or because of fear. Hundreds of people came to my grandfather's funeral, and after his death, many families came to my father to say that my grandfather had been supporting them and to ask my father to continue to do so. My grandmother never knew of the extent of her husband's charity.

Looking back, I think I had decided on my career as a therapist by the age of 9. After my grandfather died, we discovered that my grandmother had night terrors. Her daughter began sleeping in the same room with her during the week while the older grandchildren took turns staying with her during the weekends. She had to keep a light on through the night, and there were several weird looking dolls that she kept on her bed for comfort. Taking care of my grandmother made me feel grown up.

But perhaps I had decided even earlier. My father had three brothers and one sister. You could feel the tension between the brothers during every family reunion. This was while my grandparents were still alive. The family reunions abruptly stopped after my grandparents passed away. The tension among the brothers, all of whom disliked each other, ignited my interest in how to improve family relationships. How could it be that all these intelligent people couldn't sit at a table together and get along? By the time I was 12, I was reading psychology books. I was bilingual because I attended the American school, so what I couldn't get hold of in Spanish, I could read in English.

Now, in 1955, with my parents facing a huge loss, my mother relied on me once more to console my father and help him out of his severe depression. During our time in Europe, I spent many hours talking with him. My 10-year-old brother helped. He had a great sense of humor and was always the jester in the family. My 12-year-old sister was oblivious to the fact that she was in Europe, and all she wanted was to read her Nancy Drew books. As we traveled through Europe our first stop was always the American library so she could get a new book.

To this day I admire my father for his indomitable spirit. In spite of his losses, he decided to make the best of our trip to Europe. We went to Germany, where my father, using his connection to Jorge Antonio, bought a Mercedes. He insisted that we should drive up and down the Black Forest as he lectured about how the Holocaust was just an accident in history. He explained further that Germany really belonged to the Jews who had advanced the culture in so many ways and eventually Jews would go back to Germany. I didn't believe any of this. I felt the anti-Semitism wherever we went. My parents didn't speak German, but they spoke Yiddish, a language spoken exclusively by Jews. When they tried to say something in German, it came out in Yiddish, and I could feel the hatred from everyone we came in contact with.

From Germany we drove back to Paris where my mother wanted to do some shopping. She and I went to some strange places that were not actual stores, they were people's apartments where they were selling clothes at a lower price than in the stores. I don't know how she got hold of the information to do this. One time I was almost completely naked, trying something on in a small dressing room when a man came in and began to hand me things from a hook. I gasped and covered myself. He said in broken English, "Oh, don't mind me, I'm not really a man." He was gay and very funny.

After Paris we took the ferry to England. The channel was very choppy, and everyone was throwing up. We stood on the deck in the cold, and we were alright. After a few days in London, we decided to go to Stratford-on-Avon to see a Shakespeare play. On the way there we stopped for lunch in a small town. When we came out of the restaurant, our car had been stoned because we were driving a Mercedes—a German car. They probably assumed we were German. I knew that my father had bought the car for safety and convenience, but why would a Jewish family choose to drive a German car through Europe just 10 years after the war ended?

I wasn't very shocked by the stoning because by the age of 15 I was already accustomed to the many contradictions and paradoxes in life.

We went back to Paris where my father decided he would visit Zurich to meet with Ruben Antonio, Jorge's brother, to see if he could recover any of his money. He didn't want to be alone, so I went with him. He got nowhere with Ruben, and the people at the hotel treated me strangely. I realized they thought I was my father's mistress.

Prior to those three months in Europe, the five of us had never spent so much time together. I had rarely spent time around my father because he was usually working while I spent long hours at school, followed by hours with my tutors. My mother had her own interests, and my parents often went out with friends in the evening. During this trip, I had the opportunity to notice how my father constantly put down my mother. He was the smart and cultured one, whereas she didn't know anything, and my mother played along. She was Laurel to his Hardy. In the past I had noticed that he did this in the presence of friends, but now it shocked me to see him do it when his children were his only audience. My father's need to shine interfered with the happiness of the marriage.

My mother happened to be a highly intelligent and courageous woman. She and my aunt, one of my father's cousins, were the first women to attend law school in Argentina where they experienced unrelenting harassment from their fellow male students. My aunt completed her degree and went on to practice law for the rest of her life. My mother dropped out after the second year because she married my father and became pregnant with me.

My father finished law school in less than two and a half years. As a young man, he was a stutterer. He cured himself by putting stones in his mouth and forcing himself to talk, which is a technique described by Demosthenes. In Argentina at that time all the exams were oral so he probably wouldn't have been able to complete his degree had he not conquered his stuttering. He started a law practice but quit because of the rampant anti-Semitism during this time. He realized he would never be part of the aristocratic elite that controlled the profession.

During the 1930s through the end of World War II, German propaganda and Nazi ideology created a suffocating atmosphere for Jews in Argentina. Former Argentine Presidents Uriburu and Justo welcomed Nazis and their ideals. There were posters in the streets that read: "Be a patriot, kill a Jew." The University of Buenos Aires was controlled by the Argentine aristocracy, and it was very difficult for Jews to get in. The Argentinian aristocracy controlled the professions of law, medicine, and engineering. They made sure that only the surnames they approved of were admitted. That is why both of my parents went to the University of La Plata, a neighboring city about two hours away by train. During the 1930s, the University of La Plata was to Argentina what the University of California at Berkeley was to the United States during the 1960s—a place where progressive and anti-fascist students were taught by like-minded faculty.

I don't think we missed any important museum or cultural event in France, England, Italy, or Austria. I admire my parents for this, although I'm sure my mother would have rather spent more time shopping. She was very beautiful and enjoyed flaunting her beauty.

*   *   *

My parents didn't speak English, but at my insistence, we went to see the movie *East of Eden* when it opened in Paris. I fell in love with James Dean. More important, the film would eventually influence the way I think about families. Many years later, I would show the ending of the film to workshop audiences all over the world.

The film (based on a novel by John Steinbeck) is about a man who raises two sons by himself on a farm. One son is good and very close to the father. The other son, Cal, played by James Dean, can't do anything right and is constantly getting into arguments with his father. During one of those arguments, the father becomes very upset and has a stroke. The scene that I showed to my students starts when the father is lying in bed and can't speak. There is an annoying nurse in the room complaining about something, but she doesn't stay. Julie Harris, playing Abra, James Dean's girlfriend, comes in. She approaches the father's bed and says, "Please help Cal, Mr. Track. I want him to be whole and strong, and you're the only one who can do it. So try, please try. If you could ask him for something. Let him help you so that he knows that you love him. Let him do for you. Excuse me, Mr. Track, for daring to speak to you this way, but I just had to."

The father gives no sign of having heard her and she leaves the room.

James Dean comes into the room and the father moves his hand as if asking him to come close. He bends over his father's face and the father whispers, "Do something for me. That woman, the nurse, can't stand her. Don't get anybody else. You stay with me, and you take care of me."

There are tears in the son's eyes as he pulls up a chair to sit close to his father and the camera fades out and the words, "The End," appear on the screen.

This film adaptation of *East of Eden* inspired me to teach about the importance of helping parents to be able to help their children to transition from being taken care of by the parents and always being on the receiving end of the relationship, to being able to be on the giving end and help the parents, since they will inevitably be called to do this as the parents grow old. By help, I don't mean doing chores. I mean being present as adults who eventually become stronger and more knowledgeable than the parents. These ideas about how to transition through different life stages are essential to the way I think about families.

On September 30, 1955, James Dean died in a car accident, and I went into a depression. Curiously, I seemed to be more affected by what happened to a young actor who I didn't even know, than by what was happening to me and to my family. I didn't talk about it to my parents because I thought they would be offended.

Many years later, in 1973, my father would also die in a car accident at the age of 56.

*   *   *

When we were in London, we went to see Johnnie Ray, a popular singer and composer whose jazzy blues-influenced-style led the way to what would soon become rock and roll. My father said that he wanted me to see how the teenage girls in England were going crazy about a pop star and were behaving quite improperly. And, sure enough, I was shocked.

We had a box, so both the stage and the audience were visible to me. Johnnie Ray was alone on stage with his piano. He had a big head of hair that he shook as he played and sang. The audience was mostly made up of teenage girls who were dressed properly, most of them in long white dresses, but their behavior didn't match their dresses. They screamed and cried and tried to get onto the stage. Some of them looked like they were fainting. I felt I had nothing in common with these girls. Coming from Buenos Aires, I dressed in sophisticated little suits and fitted dresses, and I would never behave that way—seemingly out of control, like they did. London seemed to me old fashioned and provincial and not at all consistent with this kind of behavior.

Johnnie's most popular song was "Cry."

> "If your sweetheart sends a letter of good-bye
> It's no secret you'll feel better if you cry
> Remember sunshine can be found behind a cloudy sky
> So, let your hair down and go on and cry."

The girls let their hair down and cried. It was interesting seeing these young women publicly and overtly expressing their passion and sexual desire for the singer. It occurred to me that men would never express their emotions in this way. Since the age of 12, I had been interested in sexuality from a philosophical and psychological perspective. Simone de Beauvoir's, *The Second Sex*, was my favorite book. I also read Freud, Stekel, and Sartre, among others. These authors talked about how women suffered not only from sexual repression but also from the lack of understanding of female sexuality of those around them. I hid these books under my mattress because I knew that my father would consider them inappropriate reading for a 12-year-old and would likely confiscate them.

How did I get these books? The library and the American school obviously didn't carry them. There was an American library in downtown Buenos Aires called the Lincoln Library, which is still there. But they didn't have most of these books, so I decided to read them in Spanish. My father had found a little bookstore owned by a lady who was always there. He had made friends with her and trusted her. He told me that the chauffeur would take me to this bookstore whenever I wanted to go and that I could read anything the owner considered okay for me to read. She had no problem giving me all kinds of reading material. By the time I got to the university, I was ahead of the game.

From 1986, for more than 10 years, as director of the Family Therapy Institute of Washington DC, I ran a program that I had created for the rehabilitation of juvenile sex offenders. We had 98 percent success in preventing repeat offenses on the part of the juveniles. I believe that my interest in this subject stemmed from these early readings. I could see that male sexuality was mostly understood, but that female sexuality was a mystery. Both men and women were using sex for power, but these different levels of understanding caused them to do so in very different ways.

Seeing how the young women behaved towards Johnnie Ray made me think that times might be changing with respect to male and female sexuality.

By December, it was cold in Europe, and we went to Brazil.

CHAPTER 2

Exile

Iloved Rio de Janeiro. No city could stand in greater contrast to Buenos Aires than Rio. Where Buenos Aires was gray, grim, pessimistic, and tragic, like the tango, Rio was colorful and joyfully musical with dancing in the streets, sun, and sand.

During the five months that I lived there we moved several times from one apartment to another. At one point, we were living across the street from the beach where my brother played soccer with local boys, who he often invited over for lunch or afternoon tea. One day the janitor told my father that if my brother brought black children to the building, they would have to use the servant's entrance. In response, my father said that the whole family would only use that entrance and that's what we did from then on, even though nobody noticed and nobody cared. We had never encountered this kind of discrimination before because there were no black people in Argentina; they had all died during an epidemic in the 19th century. In Buenos Aires, we might have been told that the servants had to use the servants' entrance because they were servants, not because of the color of their skin. We were shocked by the prejudice and the injustice.

I went to the American school in Rio where I loved the teen-age parties. For the first time I learned to dance by myself, like the Brazilians did, even dancing in the streets as Carnival was approaching. The math teacher tried to persuade me to become a mathematician, but I told him I had already decided I wanted to be a psychologist.

At one point I had to stay for a few days at the home of a family with whom my father had some business. There I met the son, Miguel—22 years old, dark and handsome. He was a poet, and he would sleep most of the day and stay up at night writing poetry. I stayed up with him every night reading poetry and talking about poems and politics. We sat at the table in the dining room, speaking softly so we wouldn't wake anyone up.

We both loved Pablo Neruda, but I hated his poem "Ode to Stalin." I also disliked many of the poems he'd written when he was older. My favorite was his "Twenty Love Poems and a Song of Despair." To this day, I can recite "Poem 20" by heart, and I often do, in my head, at night when I can't sleep. Miguel was a communist and tried to make me a believer in communism and in the value of the poem "Ode to Stalin." But to no avail. I was a Marxist, but not a communist, in that I understood the conflict between labor and capital, and I was passionate about social justice, but I would never support a dictator of any kind. Those conversations late into the night were some of the happiest in my life. I had a crush on Miguel, but I knew he would never touch me because I was only 15.

One of the great gifts that my father gave me was my love for poetry. He taught me to memorize many classic Spanish poems, especially the Romantics. And to this day I still recite them to myself. I've always been good at memorizing. I think I know the words to every classic tango ever written. One of my earliest memories is of my favorite book when I was 3 years old, *Little Hiawatha*, about a little Native American boy. It was a Disney book inspired by the poem, "The Song of Hiawatha" by Henry Wadsworth Longfellow, and translated into Spanish. I had the nanny or one of my parents read it to me until I knew it by heart.

Then I would tell everyone that I knew how to read, and I would pick up the book and turn the pages exactly in the right place, showing how I could read, when I actually couldn't read at all.

I was 3 years old in 1943. It was the middle of World War II and everyone around me was sad and stressed. Perhaps this is why I felt such a need to entertain by pretending to read. I didn't quite understand what was happening, but I saw that my mother was always knitting for the soldiers, and she constantly said, "You have to eat everything in your plate because children in Europe are dying of hunger." I knew that my eating wouldn't help those children and ever since then I've had a conflicted relationship with food. By 1944 or '45, I heard that my father was on the board of the Jewish orphanage in Buenos Aires that rescued children who had escaped the Holocaust. He never talked about this, but I could tell he was going through a very difficult time.

I think I learned to read in Spanish at the age of 4 and in English at age 5. In Spanish, my favorite book was *Sophie's Misfortunes*, which was intended for children and had been translated into Spanish from French. The author was Sophie Segur, known as Countess of Segur. The story is set in a castle in the French countryside during the Second French Empire. Sophie is a naughty little girl who is very curious and adventurous and constantly making blunders. I read all of the Countess' books about little girls and their difficulties in understanding what was expected of them and how to behave. Whenever I work with little children, I remember these books. I think they helped me understand how difficult and complicated life can be for little children.

Another gift from my father has been my love of classical music. He had been a student of music theory, and as a young man, he had played the violin. One of my great memories is of when I was around 5 years old, and he took me to a performance by Arthur Rubinstein. It was just my father and I, and we sat way up front. I was transported by the music and felt so loved.

One of my favorite psychotherapy strategies is "Creating Good Memories." It applies to all ages, but it's especially good for couples. The therapist asks the couple to take turns, on a monthly basis, in creating a good memory for each other. It could be just for each other, or it could include the children. It doesn't have to involve doing something expensive or complicated, just out of the ordinary. This strategy is consistent with my way of thinking, in that sometimes it's best not to look back on old issues and try to resolve them, but instead, to look to the future and create something new.

The following year, when we moved to Uruguay, I made friends with a girl who had a beach house where Neruda had stayed and had written poems on the walls and on the shutters. Picasso had also stayed there and had painted a mural that was more valuable than the house itself. Spending time in that house somehow made me feel like I had personally known these two great artists.

*   *   *

It was May of 1956 when my parents decided it was safe enough to move to Montevideo, Uruguay. We would be closer to Buenos Aires, so family could visit and there was a large community of exiled Argentinians who helped and supported each other. I went to the French high school, which was interesting and difficult. It was there I had my first school experience of anti-Semitism. I had made friends with a girl and one day she saw me talking to two girls in the class and she admonished me: "Don't talk to those girls, they're Jewish."

"I'm Jewish too," I responded.

Her reply? "You don't look it. I would never have guessed."

That was the end of my friendship with that girl. I never put up with anti-Semitic or racist talk of any kind. I don't tolerate it when I'm working with an individual or a family, and I don't let it pass. I will call them out on it. And, of course, I don't tolerate those kinds of remarks from my students.

I made other good friends though and became close to a girl my age who was such a good artist that the most important newspaper in the country paid her to see all the plays at the National Theater and to make sketches of the actors. The drawings were published alongside the reviews of the plays. We went to the theater together regularly, and those were wonderful times.

Montevideo in those days was a beautiful, laid back, Spanish colonial town built around the port. The city sits across the River Plate (Rio de la Plata) from Buenos Aires. There were ferries that went back and forth every day and also hydroplanes. In those days the main industry in Montevideo was banking. Uruguay was called the Switzerland of South America. Today I think the main industry is tourism because of the many visitors from Argentina, Brazil, and even Europe who come to the lovely beaches. Uruguayans in those days were very educated but not trendy or fashionable like the people of Buenos Aires.

My parents quickly made friends within the exile community. My mother liked to throw parties where everyone was welcome and where she served plenty of food and wine. Still, it was hard to shake the feeling that any of us could be killed or kidnapped at any moment.

My father's family turned against him because they believed that he had known about the September coup and that's why we'd gone to Europe. They resented that he hadn't warned them so they could have also left. But the truth was that he hadn't known, and we really had gone to Europe because it was my birthday gift.

My father had three brothers and a sister. They owned shares in the family business—a factory that made car tires. As soon as we were exiled, my father's brothers refused to give him his share of the profits. One of the brothers came to visit us in Uruguay. My father insisted that I sit in on their discussions and take notes, because as his oldest daughter, he wanted me to understand how his brothers were robbing him. I suffered through those meetings, taking notes, while they quarreled bitterly. I wished that I had the skills to intervene and get them to negotiate.

The tire factory had evolved from my grandfather's raincoat and boot factory where both my parents had worked. My father ran an import-export business, and my mother opened a women's sporting wear store across the street from the raincoat store. The tire factory was an expansion of the rubber manufacturing involved in making the rain gear. My grandparents had sent the youngest son to work as a laborer at Firestone in the United States so he could learn the secrets of how to make durable tires. The factory became very successful. Eventually it expanded into an aluminum factory and was inherited by several of my cousins who continued to fight with each other.

Every time I work with a family who owns a business, I remember the conversations between my father and his brother. My father had argued that he should have his share of the profits, while my uncle insisted that my father had demonstrated that he was not responsible enough to own shares in the first place, and that's why my father was in exile. The fact that my father trusted and respected me enough to want me to sit in on these conversations made me proud and confident that someday I would be able to help others with these kinds of issues.

I loved the feeling of community among the exiles, even though we came from all walks of life and adhered to a variety of different political ideologies. One day an Argentine general, who was a Peronist, came to visit. My father, who had not quite finished getting dressed, asked me to go to the living room and entertain the general.

After welcoming him to the house, I asked him if it would be all right to pose a question.

He said, "Of course, my dear. Go ahead."

"Why are the military so stupid?" was my question.

Without missing a beat, he replied, "It's a sacrifice we make for our country."

From then on, I respected him greatly. He had given me a wonderful example of the technique of reframing, which I often teach. He'd shown no aggression or offense. He had not questioned the idea that the military are stupid. He had simply changed the purpose and meaning of the stupidity, making it a heroic sacrifice rather than a defect.

Many years later, when studying the work of Gerald Caplan in his book, *Principles of Preventive Psychiatry*, I remembered that conversation with the general. Caplan believed that the greatest challenge in training psychotherapists and other helping professionals, has to do with the prejudiced ideas they sometimes have about the people they are trying to help. For example, a teacher might think that a child with a low IQ will always be unhappy. Caplan recommends not challenging the teacher's belief, but instead pointing out other characteristics of the child. Maybe he loves to dance, to run, to play a sport. In this way the teacher is able to see new possibilities for the child. This is what the general had done. He had not challenged my belief that the military are stupid. Instead, he pointed out an admirable trait. I've taught this strategy to my students for many years.

*   *   *

After a year in Uruguay, my parents decided that it was safe for me and my siblings to go back to Buenos Aires. The military wanted our parents; they would not harm us. We returned to the house and to the American school, commuting by air every week or two to visit our parents on the weekends.

Our apartment was the second floor of a palace and it had 22 rooms. My maternal grandfather and uncle were still there, as they had always lived with us. The servants were also there. Even with people around me, I felt very uncertain, unprotected, and responsible for my younger siblings.

Many years later, when analyzing the coaching strategies of Tony Robbins, I noticed that he often asks a client, "Growing up, which parent's love did you crave the most?" He then follows up with the question, "Who did you have to be for that parent?" The answer to that question defines the person's identity and explains why she does what she does. Looking back, I realize that I felt I had my father's love. The love I craved was my mother's. For her, I had to be the caregiver, always taking care of my sister and brother, and always helping my father with his bouts of depression when his father died and after every political turmoil and every failed business. And that is what I have been all my life—the psychotherapist, the coach, the teacher—always taking care of others. I'm grateful for that. I have led a wonderful, fulfilling life. Yet it's interesting, late in life, to realize that my vocation originated in my craving for my mother's love.

My brother was rebellious and contentious. He was 11 years old when we were living in Buenos Aires without our parents, and I imagine that he found our situation very disturbing. One day he manufactured a bomb and placed it in his classroom. It didn't detonate, but we received a letter from the principal informing us that he was being expelled. I went to speak with the principal, explained my parents' situation, and told him that I would take full responsibility for my brother and that he would never do something like this again. My brother was not expelled, but that was a difficult time for me.

Often, when we visited our parents in Uruguay, my father would be traveling somewhere on business. My mother had befriended Alberto—the 20-year-old son of a family my parents knew. Their friendship included going to the movies and eating together on a regular basis. She tried to get me interested in him. I didn't like him very much, mainly because he was a friend of my mother's. He was actually quite a romantic figure who spent his time flying back and forth in small planes from Brazil to Uruguay bringing messages from Perón for his exiled followers who were hoping for his return to power.

What was confusing about Alberto was that, with the help of President Eisenhower's brother—a personal friend of his father's—he had been sent away to Cornell University at the age of 17. Alberto had become so outspoken about his dislike of Perón's government that he was an embarrassment to his father, who not only supported the regime, but was a close personal friend of Perón and his wife, Evita. Alberto's father, Luis Elias Sojit, was a well-known sports commentator on Argentine radio and he had been an old dear friend of the first lady, Eva Perón, since the time she worked as a soap opera actress. They had worked together at the radio station.

From a young age, Alberto had often been a guest at the presidential mansion where he took every opportunity to demand that jailed students be released, and that there be freedom of the press, and so on. He was very political, even at a young age. Eva Perón was fond of him. Once she took him on a train ride through small towns in the outskirts of Buenos Aires, where she was campaigning. When the train stopped at each station, there were crowds waiting to see her. Children would run to her window, and she would give them money. After a couple of stops she said to Alberto, "You're also a child. Here let me give you some money," and she put some bills on his lap. He threw the money back at her and said, "I don't want your money. I want you to free the political prisoners and the students." He was quite a character and quite outspoken.

After a couple of years at Cornell, Alberto fell ill with a kidney problem that had never been diagnosed. He was hospitalized for quite a long time, and then the revolution happened, and Luis Elias and the rest of the family went into exile, and there were no more funds for his college education. At this point, Alberto had grown so opposed to the military government that came into power after the ousting of Perón, that he decided to help the Peronist cause, even though he didn't believe in it either. Getting to know him was a lesson on how complicated everything can be and how things can be black and white at the same time—something that is invaluable for a therapist to understand.

When my father met Alberto, it was quite clear that he didn't like him. He said to me, "What I fear most about the consequences for you of this exile is that you might become close to someone with whom you're not compatible. But you're drawn to him because you've bonded over the experience of exile." Sure enough, years later I ended up marrying Alberto.

*　　*　　*

In 1956, during our stay in Uruguay, my mother invited me to go with her to Rio for a few days. It sounded like fun, and it just so happened that Alberto would be there as well. He asked me out to a night club on the Corcovado Mountain. The club was just beneath the huge statue of Christ. My mother let me go, which my father would have never allowed. The place was beautiful, with an amazing view of the whole city and the ocean. We arrived via a special cable car that only went to that night club. It was an outdoor patio under the stars with a DJ who played beautiful Brazilian music. We could see the Christ statue that was just slightly above us, while the view of Rio and the beaches spread out below. I don't think I have ever again been in such a beautiful, romantic setting.

I was wearing a white dress and Alberto was wearing a dark suit. He kept ordering rum and cokes, a fashionable drink at the time known as Cuba Libre (Free Cuba). We danced. He was not a good dancer, and I knew it was just an excuse to hold me.

Towards the end of the evening he said, "I want you to marry me."

I responded that it was a crazy idea since I was only 16 years old. I hadn't even finished high school.

He said, "You'll see, we will be married."

When I got back to my room in the hotel, I opened the white sheets on the bed and found a big cockroach sitting there. I don't believe in omens, but I remember thinking, "This is an omen." The cockroach reminded me of Sartre's novel *Nausea* and of Kafka's *The Metamorphosis*.

I was not attracted to Alberto, although he was handsome. At 6'4" he was too tall. I was only 5'2" and skinny. He was actually quite handsome. He was so handsome in fact, that when there was a film festival in Rio or in Uruguay, people would point to him in the street and call out, "Is that Gregory Peck?" Or sometimes they'd say, "That's Rock Hudson." But Alberto was not comfortable in his body. He had been an obese adolescent and he had the awkwardness of someone who grew up not liking his body.

I didn't think we had that much in common. But in so many ways we did. We were both in exile, we both spoke English, we loved American literature and jazz. Both of us had read all of Hemingway, F. Scott Fitzgerald, Arthur Miller, Walt Whitman. We were both left-leaning progressives and believed in social justice. We believed in getting as much education as we possibly could. And we were both ethnically Jewish, while identifying philosophically as atheists. We loved jazz—John Coltrane, Miles Davis, Louis Armstrong, Ella Fitzgerald, Fats Domino. Alberto had even attended the American school that I had, although only for grade school. But he was four years ahead of me, and I hadn't met him.

In spite of everything we had in common, I still thought Alberto was only interested in me for my money. I had grown up believing that nobody (with very few exceptions) liked me for myself. Everyone seemed to be interested in how they could benefit from a connection with my father, or in our weekend home, or in our beach house, or in the car and chauffeur, and so on. This limiting belief—that people are interested in me for some ulterior motive—has been with me my whole life. I also thought that my second husband wanted to marry me for my money, and that my friends and students just wanted to use me in some way. It was only when I began to work with Tony Robbins in 2002 that I learned that this is what he calls a "limiting belief," which he defines as a belief that narrows a person's choices and creates barriers between people.

I spent that summer with my family at a beach house in Uruguay. Gambling at the local casino was an elegant and popular source of entertainment in those days. My father thought that Alberto was addicted to gambling. Alberto thought he had developed a method for making a living by gambling and he was disciplined about it. He would go to the casino every day and play until he made roughly the equivalent of what would have been

50 U.S. dollars. Then he would leave. I tried to explain to my father that this was the opposite of an addiction. This was rational and disciplined, I proposed, but to no avail.

Ironically, both my parents had been addicted to gambling. Until I was 15 years old, and we went into exile, my family spent three months every summer at the beach resort of Mar del Plata, south of Buenos Aires. We rented and eventually bought a house on a corner across the street from the beach and from the golf club where my father played. Every weekend, he drove or flew back and forth from work in the city. My parents played baccarat at the upscale, fashionable casino almost every night until my father lost so much money that he decided he would never gamble again. He made my mother promise that she wouldn't gamble either, but she went to the casino almost every night during the week when my father was in the city. Sometimes he found out and I could hear him screaming at her. She was so well known at the casino that she borrowed money from the waiters when she was losing.

During the summer in Uruguay, Alberto was allowed to visit me in the house, but I was not allowed to go out with him because of our age difference. One day, he told me that they were performing a play by Arthur Miller at the national theater, and it was important for me to see it with him. After much persistence and drama, my father gave me permission to go. The play was *A View from the Bridge*. It's about a man who is sexually attracted to his young niece. The play was first produced in New York in 1955, at a time when incest and sexual abuse were taboo subjects.

At the end of the play, Alberto said, "This is how your father feels about you. It's disgusting, but don't worry, I will always be there to protect you from him."

I knew that this was just a ploy on Alberto's part to make himself important in relation to me. He was going to save me from my father, who had never done anything inappropriate (although I knew he was intensely emotionally involved with me). Yet Alberto's words planted a seed of doubt in my mind about my father's love for me. I knew that my father's intention was to love and protect me. Yet this love often seemed to me to be intrusive, possessive, and dominating. Many years later, in my book, *Sex, Love, and Violence*, I wrote about how easily love can turn into violence.

My parents were never physically abusive. They both abhorred violence, but my father screamed a great deal. I can't remember my mother ever raising her voice. My father actually taught me how to shout to command authority. He said he had learned to do this during his military service.

*   *   *

At 14 years old, I was one of the very few Argentine girls going to the American school. The American girls had all kinds of freedoms that I was not permitted to have. I lived between two worlds. I was very much part of the American culture, but I didn't really belong because my parents didn't speak English and never set foot in my school. This feeling of not belonging has stayed with me throughout my entire life. Many years later, coming back to the United States from a trip abroad, the U.S. customs officer looked at my passport and said, "Welcome home." I remember thinking that is so nice. Maybe this is my home; maybe I belong here.

One day I was invited to a teenage party on a Saturday evening at a church near my school. I knew my father wouldn't let me go, but I also knew that my parents would be out that evening. So, I convinced my uncle, who lived with us, to drive me to the party and pick me up at a reasonable time. The party was unpleasant. I could feel I had nothing in common with the kids there. I felt overdressed in my white dress. A boy asked me to dance, and as we danced, suddenly I felt a huge repulsion towards him. I excused myself and went to the bathroom and just stood there.

A girl came up to me and asked if there was anything wrong.

I explained that I just wanted to get away from the boy I was dancing with.

She told me that I had done the right thing and that he had raped a girl at a party a couple of weeks earlier.

I felt a great sense of solidarity with that girl. I stayed in the bathroom until it was time to meet my uncle.

When I got home, I went to the butler's office—a small room next to the informal dining room where we could get water and a snack. I was getting water when my father came in.

He said, "You're wearing lipstick." I had forgotten to take it off.

He started screaming, "I told you you're not allowed to wear lipstick," and other things I don't remember.

He picked up a glass and threw it in my direction as if he were trying to hit my face, but it shattered against the wall. I was frozen in fear.

At that moment my nanny came running in, grabbed him by the shirt, shook him violently and screamed, "Don't you ever touch her. Don't you ever dare to touch her." This was said using the familiar second person pronoun *vos* instead of the formal *usted.*

He pulled himself away and left.

She told me to go to sleep, and that she'd pick up the glass.

I went to my room, walking through the servants' quarters because I was afraid of running into my father in the other wing of the apartment. After that incident I was convinced that he had been sexually intimate with the nanny. Otherwise, she would have never grabbed him like that, or addressed him using the familiar Spanish pronoun. So that was another puzzlement: Why would my father be having a sexual relationship with my nanny—a poor girl who had been working for us since she was 16? I knew that this was abuse of power. I had suspected for quite some time that my father slept around with many women, but this was still a shock. Also, if he loved me, why would he pretend he was throwing a glass at my face? Was he pretending or did he really intend to harm me? And why would he want to harm me for wearing lipstick? What would have happened if the nanny hadn't come into the room? I still loved my father, but I would never trust him again. I never spoke about this to anyone, not even to my analyst during my six years of psychoanalysis.

Looking back, I realize that later in life, when I worked for many years with violent men, this experience helped me to understand how many of them could love a woman, and at the same time, want to hurt her.

One of my favorite pieces of literature is Franz Kafka's *Letter to His Father*. As a grown woman, I've wanted to write my own "Letter to My Father." I had no desire to blame him; I just would have liked for him to explain himself.

CHAPTER 3

Evita

It was my senior year of high school at the American Community School. It was 1958, and my parents had decided that it was safe enough for them to return to Buenos Aires.

One day, the principal called me to his office to ask when I would be applying to college in the U.S. All my classmates were filling out applications and he'd assumed that I would be applying as well. I told him my parents weren't going to let me go. They thought it was too far away for a girl to be on her own without her family. He asked where I would want to go if I did have permission. I answered, "Radcliffe." At that time, women were not allowed into Harvard, the most renowned American university, but they could attend Radcliffe, Harvard's sister school.

The principal told me that I would get in. "I know," I said. "Would it be possible for me to ask for a scholarship? I think if I got in with a scholarship, maybe my father would be impressed and let me go."

But the principal said that everyone knew my father was wealthy, and everyone knew he could afford to pay.

I promised him that I would return the scholarship as soon as

I got it. He agreed to let me apply for a scholarship. Later that year I was awarded a scholarship from Radcliffe, but still my father didn't let me go.

My life would probably have been much easier had I gone to Radcliffe. Still today, it hurts that I didn't get to go. But I also think that perhaps because I didn't go to Radcliffe, I had to work extra hard to prove myself. Maybe if had I gone, I would not have fulfilled my ambition to make a contribution to psychology. Sometimes when you have to struggle, you ultimately succeed beyond your initial goals.

Today I realize that I was too obedient and submissive. If this happened today to an 18-year-old girl at the American school in Buenos Aires, she would make so much trouble that her family would be in therapy and probably the therapist would intercede in her favor. But there was no family therapy in those days. I realized that my parents were ignorant about the importance of an education at Radcliffe. I also knew that in great part this was because I was a girl and I would get married, so education would not matter anyway. I had these thoughts at the time, and they influenced why I became a family therapist years later. I wanted adolescent girls to be heard and I wanted them to be able to fulfill their dreams.

By the time I was in my 20s, I realized that my timidity and submissiveness had affected my younger siblings who had grown up watching me. I couldn't go anywhere and very few friends were acceptable. Neither of my parents was interested at all in what happened at my school. If I brought home a friend and my mother took a dislike to her, she would be rude and even cruel to the girl. I know now from experience with families that my sister and brother decided that they would be the opposite of how I was. This is a typical reaction of the younger siblings to an older child who is too well behaved. My siblings became very rebellious and extreme. My sister ran away at age 16. She lived at a girlfriend's house and got a job teaching English at a school by lying about her age. When she came back, she frequently sneaked her boyfriend into her bedroom where he would spend the night. My brother was perpetually getting into trouble—especially at the beach house—during the summers where he had all kinds of people sleeping in our garage.

Since I couldn't go to college in the United States, I had to get into the University of Buenos Aires. The Argentine Department of Education did not accept the American high school as equivalent to the Argentine high school, so I had to study all of Argentine history, literature, and geography and pass a series of exams before I could get into the university. This was a huge cause of anxiety for me. To this day, I have a recurring nightmare about how all my degrees and accomplishments are canceled because I didn't go to the proper high school.

Our high school principal had been a kind and caring person, but my relationship with the school had not always been good. When I was 5 years old, my parents decided that I would go to first grade at the American Grammar and High School, which later became the American Community School, and eventually Lincoln School. They wanted me to be fluent in English. They hired the principal of the school—a Christian fundamentalist—to teach me the language as a private tutor. I wanted to go to an Argentine school where the hours were just in the morning as opposed to the American school, which had a full day schedule ending at 3:00 p.m., just like in the U.S. What I dreaded most, because I was a picky eater, was to have to eat lunch at school. I made my mother promise to pick me up so I could have lunch at home.

On the first day, the children were told to form two lines—one for those who were going home for lunch and the other for those who were eating at school. I went to the line for going home, and I stood on the sidewalk until everyone had left and I was alone. A teacher came out and said that I was supposed to eat at school. She took me to the dining room where she sat me at the principal's table. The principal put some food on my plate and told me to eat it. I said, "No, thank you." She forced me to eat it, and as soon as I had swallowed, the food came up and I threw up on my plate. To my terror and profound embarrassment, she forced me to eat my vomit in front of everyone.

From that day on, I knew that the principal was intent on breaking my spirit and I lived in fear of her. Also, from that day on, I made the key decision never to trust my mother. Many years later I wrote about key decisions in my book, *Relationship Breakthrough*. A key decision (a term coined by Tony Robbins) is a decision made under traumatic circumstances, usually in early childhood, that typically has negative consequences, but at the moment, helps to maintain the integrity of the child. In order to understand a key decision, you have to understand what happened before the key decision was made. In my case what happened was that my mother had promised to pick me up and she didn't. I would never trust her again. The obvious consequence was that I didn't think she loved me, and I would not rely on her or believe her for many years.

But maybe I had made this key decision earlier. I think I was 3 years old when I was riding my tricycle around the apartment, and I fell. My mother picked me up, and not in a gentle way, put me on a bed and said, "Look what you've done! Your ear is all red and swollen and now we have to go to a birthday party with you looking like that." My ear was hurting and all she cared about was how I would look at the party.

Later on, I realized that my mother cared very much about physical beauty, and I suspected that I was not as pretty as she would have wanted me to be, but that my sister was. In early adolescence my sister's beauty enabled her to have a special bond with my mother, and her extraordinary looks distorted the way I saw myself. When I look at old pictures, I realize that I was quite attractive, but at the time, I didn't think so. My sister was Elizabeth Taylor, as my father used to call her, and I was Jane Powell, as he called me. My mother was gorgeous, an Ava Gardner type, for those who remember Ava Gardner—black hair, very light skin, beautiful green eyes, a mole right next to her upper lip, a tiny waist, and big breasts. I remember once when I was about 8 years old, she was putting on make-up and I asked her, "Mommy do you think I'm pretty?" Her answer was, "You have beautiful eyes." To me that meant that she thought the only pretty thing about me was my eyes.

Alberto's mother told me that when my mother was young, she lived on the same block as she and her family did. My mother had been so beautiful that when she came out of the house the neighbors would go to the windows to look at her. She was also very elegant even though the family was quite poor.

I have other difficult memories going back to when I was 3 years old. At the time, my father became severely ill with asthma, and he sat all day long in the middle of the living room covered in blankets. He could hardly speak. I rode my tricycle wildly around him. I was so anxious I could have climbed the walls. To this day, when I see a "hyperactive" child, I know that the anxiety is because of concern about someone else in the family, and the hyperactivity comes from the despair of not being able to help. When my father got better and could talk, he would say, "Now Cloé—the bad one—will go away." And I would hide behind a heavy drape. Then he would say, "Now Diana—the good one—will come out." And I would walk towards him smiling like a little angel. My middle name is Diana.

This strategy of dissociation is useful in getting rid of un-wanted parts of the personality by developing a different persona. In therapy, it can be helpful to ask a person to describe a part of themselves that is happy, or wiser, or loving, and to give that part a name. Then, by using the name, that different self can come forward. It's a way of helping someone to develop a stronger identity. This strategy was developed by Milton Erick-son, a prominent psychiatrist and hypnotist. The same strategy is used by Tony Robbins at his events in his interventions with individuals.

Years later, I was able to understand my mother and forgive her. Her own mother had died when my mother was 10 years old, and I think she didn't want to love us too much for fear that she would die and that we would not be able to overcome the grief. She was a very good mother when I grew up and had children of my own.

I was deeply affected by my parents' refusal to let me go to Radcliffe. This was so painful to me that I couldn't talk about it at all and never brought it up again. I have always understood why it's often the case that people can't talk about the most difficult events in their lives. Talking brings the experience to life and reliving it can be unbearably painful.

I did eventually talk to my mother about the Radcliffe trauma. It happened many years later, when I lived in the United States, and she was visiting from Argentina during a time when I was busy helping one of my daughters with her college applications. One day, my mother made a comment about how stressful the process seemed. I was able to say, "Remember when I got into Radcliffe and you and Dad didn't let me go?" She had no memory of this. To her it was a non-event. That is how distant my mother had been from me. But it was also the case that my parents had been part of a different world both culturally and geographically. They couldn't even have imagined sending their teenaged daughter off to study anywhere as far away as Boston. They didn't understand that I would have been guaranteed a completely different kind of future.

The abusive principal continued to be my tutor (and my siblings' tutor as well) until the third or fourth grade. I don't know how it was that my parents didn't realize that the teachers and the students knew that she came regularly to our house, and this caused social problems for us. In my first year of high school, an English teacher gave us an assignment that consisted of reading a story about a British spinster in the 19th century, and we had to write a character analysis of the protagonist. When she returned my paper, I had a "D." I asked her, in front of the class, why I was given a "D". She said it was because I had not written that paper; it was clear that someone else had written it for me. I don't know what she was thinking because my parents didn't even speak English. Maybe she thought that Miss Salibian, the abusive principal, had written it. I said to her, "Give me something to write about and I will write another paper here, in front of the classroom, on the subject that you give me." I wrote the essay, and she gave me an "A." The key decision I made then has had good consequences for the rest of my life. I don't let anyone put me down.

*   *   *

Juan Perón was elected President of Argentina three times, serving from June 1946 to September 1955, when he was overthrown in a coup, and then from October 1973 until his death in July 1974. During his first presidential term (1946-1952), Perón was supported by his second wife, Eva Duarte (Evita). The couple was immensely popular among the Argentine working class. The Perón's followers admired their efforts to eliminate poverty and to dignify labor, while their detractors considered them demagogues and dictators.

Evita, coming from humble origins, was loathed by the elite but adored by the poor for her work with the sick, the elderly, and orphans. It was due to her behind-the-scenes work that women's suffrage was granted in 1947. She introduced social justice and equality into the national discourse. She stated: "It is not philanthropy, nor is it charity… It is not even social welfare. To me it is strict justice… I do nothing but return to the poor what the rest of us owe them, because we have taken it from them unjustly."

Evita is still considered a saint by many Argentines because of her work for the poor. Juan Perón was a populist— a democratically elected president who silenced the opposition, committing many human rights abuses, particularly against university students. It was rumored that Evita was involved in abuses against the upper classes, who she called the *oligarchy*.

In 1948, Evita established the Eva Perón Foundation with the purpose of helping poor children, building homes, schools, hospitals, and orphanages. By the end of the 1940s, the Foundation had funds of over 3 billion pesos, controlled 200 million on the exchange rate, employed over 14,000 workers, purchased 500,000 sewing machines, 400,000 pairs of shoes, and 200,000 cooking pots for distribution annually, and had built numerous houses, schools, hospitals, and orphanages. She was Robin Hood—taking from the rich and giving to the poor.

There were allegations that most of the foundation's wealth was ill-gotten, with Evita coercing people into donating. One of these people was my father.

When my grandfather died, my father inherited a considerable amount of money and purchased a large department store in the center of the city, across the street from Harrods—the Argentine branch of the famous department store in London. The store was quickly remodeled. My mother became the buyer and the decorator. Both my parents worked long hours and the store became a big success.

One day, my father received a letter signed by Eva Perón, thanking him for his generous donation of the store to the union of white-collar workers. My father knew that if he didn't donate the store, she might have him tortured and killed. He met with Evita multiple times over several weeks, trying to convince her that she should pay him a fair price for the store, or at least pay him something instead of just confiscating it.

I wasn't sure what was going on, but I knew it was something very bad for my father and for our family. He was very sickly and developed a stomach ulcer during that time. I lived in fear that something horrible was about to happen. I developed a kind of mantra that I would say to my father every morning. It was something like, "I hope everything goes well for you today, the way you want it." I was hoping that my words would make some magic happen.

Then the day came when he was supposed to make the donation to the union. It was a big event with hundreds of people in a theater and Evita and my father were on the stage. She said to him, "You go first. Announce your donation and then I'll say a few words."

My father responded, "No, we have to stick to protocol: ladies go first. Then, after you, I will say some words."

She agreed and addressed the audience explaining that my father—out of his extraordinary generosity and kindness—was giving his treasured department store as a donation to the union. The audience applauded and cheered.

Then it was his turn to speak. He said, "The lady is very kind, but she exaggerates. This gift is her gift to you. She compensated me generously out of her own money and now she is giving this store to you. Please express your gratitude."

The audience went crazy. Everyone stood up and cheered for Evita. Many people cried. Evita looked at my father, and she said, "Touché." And she paid him. She had no choice. She couldn't disappoint her followers and contradict my father, who seemed so truthful in expressing his admiration for her generosity. Also, there were many reporters in the room who would have reported on any disagreement regarding whose donation it really was. The coverage would not have been favorable to her.

Yes, I think being strategic is in my genes.

Perón borrowed our Mercedes convertible when there was a parade because it was bigger than the presidential car. When Evita was so sick that she couldn't even sit, they put her in a cast to hold up her body and paraded her through the streets to show the populace that she was still alive.

I will never forget the day she died. I was alone in the family room watching television when suddenly the screen went black and after a few minutes the voice of an announcer came on: "Today, at 19:20, Eva Perón has passed into immortality. There will be no radio or television for the next seven days." Then the screen went blank. I went into my parents' room where my mother was taking a nap and told her. She said we all knew this was going to happen, and that it was all right. But I was in shock. It was remarkable to grow up as a girl in a country where the most powerful person was a beautiful 24-year-old woman and then have her die at age 32. Although I knew about the many bad things she had done, I was still filled with grief.

She had planned to steal from my father, and then, some years later, we were persecuted and had to go into exile because my father was considered a Peronist. But these contradictions were commonplace in my life.

When Perón fell, there were three years of military rule under Aramburu, who in 1958 decided to allow free elections and Arturo Frondizi was elected president. The Peronist party had been banned and Juan Perón was not permitted to return to Argentina from his exile. My parents came home to Buenos Aires. Alberto and his family also returned, and we continued our friendship. But now the friendship was becoming a romance.

President Frondizi was a well-educated intellectual and the University of Buenos Aires flourished under him, which was very fortunate for me. Many professors who had left during the Peronist era and the subsequent military dictatorship, came back.

Still, in many ways, Arturo Frondizi was nothing more than a puppet of the military dictatorship that preceded him. The reason he was able to get elected was that the most popular political party— the Peronist party—had been banned. Even the mention of the name Perón had been prohibited and could land you in jail. There was no real democracy in Argentina, and this suited the interests of the U.S. government very well. During the Cold War, the U.S. supported dictatorships all over Latin America out of fear of Soviet expansion. The thinking was that wherever real democratic elections take place, there exists the possibility that the communist party could be elected to power, which would further Soviet expansion.

When I finished high school, I had been determined to study psychology. The problem was that at that time there was no department of psychology in Buenos Aires. I decided I would become a psychiatrist, although I didn't really want to go through medical school. Having to get through medical school seemed absurd for what I was interested in—understanding why people do what they do.

My father was also opposed to medical school. His view was that his daughter was not going to work with dead bodies in the morgue. During the first year of medical school in Argentina, one has to take anatomy and work with body parts.

"The important decision that you have to make," said my father, "is whether you want to make a living from your capital or from your labor."

"From my labor," I said. "I want to help people and I want to make a contribution to the field of psychology. I want to understand why people do the things they do and how to help them to have better lives."

Somewhat predictably, he countered, "Life is easier when you live off of your capital."

Underlying this conversation was my contempt for what I considered the bourgeois life and the ambitions of my parents. I disliked the way they relied on material possessions and what I considered a frivolous lifestyle for fulfillment. My mother told me that the anti-Semitism of the 1930s had pushed my father into being a merchant when what he had wanted to be was a lawyer—a repeat of centuries of history for the Jews. He was a lawyer, but, as a Jew, he would never be accepted into the elite judicial circles.

"I understand that you want to have a career and you want to be a professional," said my father, "but why does it have to be about the most sordid aspects of life—the suffering, disturbed people? Couldn't you go into the arts instead. Couldn't you work with things of beauty instead of the most sordid?"

"I want to devote myself to solving the most difficult questions," I explained. "Why do people do what they do? Why is there so much violence and cruelty? These are the most important questions, and this is what I'm going to do."

Meanwhile, Alberto had decided to go into economics and

was putting tremendous pressure on me to go to school with him. He had already taken many classes from the Department of Economics at Cornell University. I wasn't interested in economics, because in those days, the main premise in that field was that people behave rationally and I knew that this wasn't true. I felt that the entire discipline was based on a false premise.

Ultimately, I gave in and studied economics with Alberto for one year. In hindsight I realize that I was repeating the same timidity and submissiveness I'd shown towards my parents when they wouldn't allow me to go to Radcliffe. Alberto worked, so he didn't have as much time to study as I did. He wasn't happy that I was getting better grades. All the exams were oral. The student had to stand in front of three professors who were sitting behind a desk on a platform above the student. One of the professors rolled a bingo type of devise and a number came up that randomly matched a number in the syllabus of the subject of the class. The student had to extemporaneously talk about that subject. The professors could interrupt with questions at any point. My father coached me on how to take these exams. Whatever the subject was, he said to study really well the two or three items at the beginning of the syllabus. Then, if I was asked about something that came later, I was to explain that in order to understand C, we'd have to go back to understanding A and B. That strategy was brilliant and helped me many times, not only to pass exams, but to get A's in them.

After a year, the University of Buenos Aires added a department of psychology. The newly minted department shared a building with the philosophy, sociology, and comparative literature departments. Jorge Luis Borges was a member of the university faculty during that time. I told Alberto that switching to psychology was something that I just had to do. He was upset and became jealous and possessive. He began to talk about marriage, although we didn't have the means to support ourselves.

In 1958, Frondizi enacted policies that permitted YPF (Yacimientos Petroliferos Fiscales, or Argentine Fiscal Oil Fields) to grant rental contracts to foreign firms, allowing them to access new wells, fostering an expansion of exploration and oil production. On several occasions, my father traveled to the U.S. to assist in the negotiation of these contracts with U.S. firms.

My father—who was still opposed to my relationship with Alberto—decided to invite me along with my mother on one of his trips. The idea was that the trip might open new possibilities for me and lead me to break up the relationship with Alberto. My mother went along with this, although she very much wanted to marry me off as soon as possible. I think she feared that I might lose my virginity before marriage.

My father left for New York first. My mother and I were to stop in Miami for a few days before meeting him in New York.

CHAPTER 4

The FBI

We arrived in Miami. My mother wanted nothing more than to go shopping. She bought clothes for me, my sister, and herself. We shopped for three days and then flew to New York City. My father was busy negotiating American investments in Argentine oil, so I was stuck with my mother, who was still only interested in shopping.

On the second day, at one of the large department stores, the sales lady said she had to find change for my mother and disappeared for a long time. She came back with a security officer, and we were arrested with no explanation. We were taken to a police station where I was separated from my mother and searched by a female officer, still without explanation. She had me take off the white dress I was wearing (fortunately, I didn't have to take off my underwear). When I was dressed again, the officer took me to another room where they took a mug shot of me. It reminded me of the movies. I thought all of this was mysterious and exciting. I wasn't afraid because I knew my father was going to get us out of there. This had to be a huge misunderstanding of some kind. After I sat in a small office room for about half an hour, the same female officer came in and said that an FBI agent was coming to take me to my hotel. I asked her about my mother, and she said another agent had already left with her for the hotel.

The FBI agent was a handsome young man in a gray suit. I wondered whether he was carrying a gun. He said we had to go quickly and quietly through a back door because there might be reporters waiting for us in the front of the building. Once we were a couple of blocks away from the police station, he introduced himself and explained he was a lawyer working for the FBI. My mother had been using fake $100 bills to shop in Miami and in New York. When we were arrested, she called my father, who asked his contacts in the U.S. government to get us released. I was thrilled to be walking through Manhattan on a summer evening as the sun was setting, with a charming, handsome FBI agent who seemed genuinely interested in me, particularly in how well I spoke English.

When I got to the hotel, my mother was already there. The FBI had searched our rooms and found all the change from the $100 bills that my mother had kept in a drawer. My father didn't say a word to me, nor did he, as far as I could tell, say anything to my mother. I didn't want to ask for an explanation for fear of what I might find out. Later my mother told me that my father had unknowingly bought a few thousand dollars of fake $100 bills from some shady exchange dealer. When he realized they were fake, he gave them to my mother and asked her to burn them. She did not do it, and instead, decided to use them for shopping in the United States. The incident put my father in a particularly awkward position with his American contacts.

I enjoyed New York and was happy that my parents decided to ignore the counterfeit money episode and behave as if it hadn't happened. They didn't say a word about it and neither did I. We visited the sites and even went to see some wonderful theater productions. My favorite of these was Arthur Miller's *The Crucible,* which was performed in a small roundabout theater. My parents—my father in particular—desperately tried to understand and kept whispering to me to translate for them. I tried to translate, but I couldn't without disturbing the audience.

We ate at some great restaurants. Once, at a dark, romantic Hawaiian themed restaurant called Trader Vic's, my father asked me, "What do you see that's special and different here?"

"They're all couples," I said.

"Yes, and what's special about these couples?"

"They are quiet," I said. "It doesn't seem like they're talking to each other."

"That's right. Good observation," said my father. "It would never be this quiet at a restaurant in Buenos Aires." Of course, this was the 1950s. Things are different now in New York. He loved the United States, especially American democracy and the checks and balances between the different political institutions. Our love for the U.S. was something important that we had in common.

My father probably thought that the quietness in the restaurant was strange because he was usually talkative and entertaining. He had always been fascinated by intricacies of communication. He introduced me not only to the nuances and complexities in poetry but also in conversations. He liked to have fun with what he understood about human discourse and language.

Once, on the way to a party, he asked me if I wanted to see how he could get people to treat me strangely.

"Okay, but don't embarrass me," I hesitated.

The guests at the party were mostly people who hadn't met me. My father went around the room introducing me by saying, "This is Cloé. She's the daughter from my first marriage."

I was, in fact, the daughter from his first marriage. But his first marriage was his only marriage. People looked at me strangely and weren't sure how to deal with me. He had demonstrated how you could change the way someone responds to you simply by changing one or two words in your communication so that you are creating uncertainty around the facts surrounding someone's identity.

Once we were waiting for a table at a restaurant in Punta del Este, a beach resort in Uruguay where we frequently vacationed. The restaurant was full of people we knew. My father gave a false name for the reservation—Mr. Lopez. When the table was ready, they called out repeatedly on the loudspeaker, "Mr. Lopez," and all the people we knew looked at him, disconcerted as he walked by because they knew that wasn't his name.

I remember that when Jewish charities would ask him for money, he would say, "I gave already, but my brother Manuel hasn't. Here is his phone number."

To this day, when I feel compelled to work too hard, I say to myself, "I don't need to do this. I gave already."

My parents both knew how to enjoy themselves. They had a certain *joie de vivre*, which I also have and I'm grateful for that.

* * *

In 1958, at the beginning of the Frondizi presidency, when my father was away on a business trip, an unexpected visitor rang the doorbell. The butler couldn't understand him because he spoke in English, so he asked my mother and me to come to the door. The man introduced himself, and gave my mother his card, explaining that he was a businessman who had met my father in Brazil. My father had mentioned having an 18-year-old daughter who was completely bilingual. He wanted to know if he could enlist my help for an hour or two, to be an interpreter during an important and delicate business meeting.

My mother asked me if I wanted to do this and of course I said yes. It sounded like an adventure. I grabbed my coat and left with him. He had a professional driver for his car. After he closed the door and we were already moving, he told me we needed to make a quick stop at his hotel, the Alvear Palace, because he had to make a phone call and pick up his briefcase. I told him that was fine. Instead of having me wait in the lobby of the hotel, he asked me to come up to his room. I agreed to go up to the room with him, although by now I was getting suspicious. Inside the room I quickly took a seat at the desk so I could be near a phone in case I had to call security. My apprehensions about his possible advances turned out to be unwarranted. He never came near me. He made a quick call from the second phone by the bed, assured the person on the other end that everything was all right, grabbed his briefcase, and we were on our way.

We arrived at a nondescript office building in downtown Buenos Aires that seemed empty. He led me to a nondescript meeting room. Two men were already in the room and the conversation began. The two men spoke only Spanish. Translating for the three of them was easy in the sense that they spoke slowly and waited for me to translate. But it was difficult because I quickly realized that they didn't want me to really understand what they were talking about. It took me several minutes to register that they were talking about sending weapons to Fidel Castro, coming from the U.S. and going through Argentina. They used words like "merchandise," but several times they slipped and mentioned military equipment and weapons. I couldn't tell if the weapons were coming from an American manufacturer or from the U.S. government. Castro was in the mountains in Cuba fighting to overthrow the American supported dictator Fulgencio Batista. I was somewhat shocked, but not much, considering what my life had been like up to that point.

When my father came home, he was outraged and angry at my mother for letting me go. He said he had never met that man. But why had he wanted me in particular? There were plenty of translators at the Alvear Palace Hotel. Probably this meeting had been so secret that he couldn't risk using an official translator who could have leaked information to the press or to whoever else might have been interested.

Recently, as I was preparing to write this memoir, I mentioned this anecdote to a friend. "Your parents were friends with the American ambassador and his wife, right?" he asked.

When I affirmed that, the friend continued, "So, this was someone from the U.S. military who asked the ambassador for an innocent, trustworthy translator, and the ambassador instructed him on how to get to your house and approach your mother."

My friend's theory makes sense. My only possible connection to this kind of meeting must have been through the U.S. ambassador. The United States had been arming Castro. Of course, he later became the arch enemy of the U.S. and is suspected by some to have been responsible for John Kennedy's assassination.

*　*　*

When we lived in the palace, we had two butlers. One was Basilio, a Russian who came with the house. We inherited him from the previous tenants, who had brought him from Russia. We loved him even though he was a little crazy. He meticulously cleaned every room in the reception area. The chambermaid cleaned the bedrooms and bathrooms. Basilio loved the antique ivory and porcelain things that my mother had in the living room. He cleaned them every day while he talked to them. He also made and served breakfast every morning for people as they were getting up. To reach the breakfast room, you had to walk by the reception area (meaning the living room, dining room, study, and gallery), and you could hear him conversing with the objects. He also fixed whatever was broken, and he constantly complained that my mother wouldn't buy new appliances or even replace the parts on the appliances we already owned. Once we were having lunch and he came into the room. The motor of the washing machine could be heard from where we sat and he said to my father in his heavy Russian accent, "I can't tolerate this anymore. We need a new motor." This was actually a complaint about my mother not wanting to buy a new machine, even though he didn't say it directly.

Basilio was always there for whatever we needed. He lived in the male servant quarters on the ground level of the building, and we could call him up at any time. The other butler was a tall, handsome young man. He served the table with impeccable manners and always wore white gloves with his uniform. He taught me how to peel an orange without touching it with my hands, and he explained all the intricacies of how to serve yourself when he passed around a tray—what fork to use, what glass to drink from, and so on. He did not leave the room while we ate. He stood there waiting in case someone needed something. My parents threw frequent dinner parties for many guests. It was fine for him to stand there during the parties. But when it was just our family, we had a tendency to get into arguments at the table, and it was awkward for us to have him there.

My father sat at the head of the table and my grandfather sat at the other end. Whenever we started quarreling, I could see my grandfather's hand go to his ear. He would turn off his hearing aide, then continue eating unperturbed. I usually argued with my father about my lack of freedom and my many restrictions. Sometimes he would pick up a knife from the table, hand it to me with the blade pointing to himself, and say, "Stab me. It would hurt me less." At other times he would say, "You have to tell me that in writing. Send me a letter." After he died, I found a file labeled "Cloé," which contained all the hateful letters he had saved.

There was a beautiful young maid who served at the dinner parties, and I sometimes heard her coming from the dining room complaining that some dinner guest had pinched her behind. The parties usually started at 9:00 p.m. The nanny had to dress us up to meet the guests for five minutes and then take us to bed. As I grew older, I was told to stay a little longer to talk with the guests, but I don't think I was ever invited to sit at the table. When I was in high school, my father would sometimes have me explain one of my school essays—usually about current events—to the guests. Our family and close friends always ate at an adjacent dining room. The formal dining room was reserved for parties.

There was a huge guest bathroom with a beautiful antique vanity and a rug that was a polar bear, with the actual head and claws. Often the women at the parties would all get up and go to the bathroom together. I could see them taking turns to throw up in the toilet. Bulimia already existed back then, or maybe it's always been around. Many years later it would become one of my specialties as a therapist. Maybe it was easy for me to understand bulimics because I had known many of them early on in life.

I had my own control issues around the topic of food. My mother had been somewhat obsessed with food, perhaps because she had grown up poor. Ever since I was very young, she forced me to eat. The more she wanted me to eat, the less I ate. To this day I can't even taste polenta because she forced me to eat it so many times. Fortunately, most of the time I ate with the servants, and they didn't force me to eat anything.

Then there was the cook who made lunch, afternoon tea, and dinner. I hardly ever set foot in the kitchen. My mother would get up at around 10:00 or 11:00 and meet with the cook to discuss the day's meals. Each meal had to be at least three courses, always including fresh vegetables and a dessert. The cook was also a pastry chef, and my mother expected fresh cakes and pastries every afternoon and usually creamy French style desserts for dinner. In those days, it was thought that sugar was good for children because it went straight to the brain. We could invite as many friends to eat at the house as we wanted, and there was always enough for everyone. Also, if we came home late at night from a party with one or several friends, the cook and Basilio were always ready and willing to prepare a meal.

I describe the servants who were in our lives because they were important in my formative years. As a young woman, I was impressed by the movie, *The Servant*, written by Harold Pinter, which came out in 1963. It's a study in upper class impotence and the dynamics of personal power politics. It dramatizes the powerlessness of the powerful—a theme that runs through all my work as a family therapist.

The nanny, Gilda, was part Quechua Indian, although she was very fair. and her eyes were green because her father was of

Spanish descent. She came to work as my nanny when she was 16 years old, before my sister was born. She was very loving, but she missed her family and she cried frequently because of her boyfriends. When she cried, she said she was going to kill herself. Before we lived in the palace, we used to spend every weekend at a country club where we had an apartment and where my father played golf and my mother played cards. A well-known psychoanalyst was also a member. My mother would laugh whenever she recounted the time when this psychoanalyst told her that she should get closer to me because I was so close to the nanny that I was beginning to look more like her than like my mother. Even as a child, I couldn't understand how my mother thought this was funny, instead of taking it seriously. Being raised by a somewhat indifferent mother and a suicidal nanny definitely made me stronger and prepared me for being a successful therapist.

Somewhere between the ages of 7 and 9, my mother let me tag along with Gilda on her days off to visit with her family who worked for another family and lived in the servants' quarters. I was shocked by the sordidness of their living conditions. I thought it was irresponsible of my mother to let me go, but it was a fascinating learning experience in terms of seeing the gross inequalities in the society in which we lived. I realized then that it's one thing to look at poverty from the outside, but it's another to actually spend time with the poor as they go about their daily lives. One day my nanny said to me, "I think it's better to grow up poor rather than rich. When I was a child, I didn't have to learn English and French and play the piano. I didn't go to school all day, like you do. I spent all day playing outside." I thought it was interesting that she could see a positive side to growing up poor.

Gilda was very funny. She would come into our room in the morning to wake us up to go to school. First, she would pull open the heavy brocade curtains to let the light come in. Then she would leave for a few minutes and come back with a glass of chocolate milk for each of us, which she placed on the nightstands. I never wanted to drink it because it made me nauseous. She would say, "If you don't drink just a little bit, your mother will be angry with me. She thinks you need the sugar for your brain." If we still didn't get up, she would start pulling at our pajama pants until we got up. This ritual played out every day.

One day I was upset because I hadn't gotten the dress I wanted for a party at the school. Gilda began to tug at the curtains and performed an imitation of the servant in *Gone with the Wind*. She said, "Don't be upset, Missy. I will make you a beautiful dress from these curtains." I laughed.

A therapy strategy that I developed many years later, which I called "Riches of the Poor," was inspired by the things I learned from Gilda. The first time I used this strategy was during a recession in the U.S. A family came for therapy at my institute, ostensibly because two of their children were fighting, but the real problem was with the parents. The father had worked as a janitor all his life and was suddenly fired from his job. He felt humiliated because now the family was on food stamps, and he couldn't find work. The mother had developed MS and could hardly walk into the therapy room. I observed from behind a one-way mirror as they talked to the therapist, and I realized that the most important thing to do was to restore dignity to the family. I told the therapist to say, "There are many ways to be rich. One way is to have money, but there are other ways. I want to go around the circle and have each of you tell me how your family is rich, even though you don't have much money." The response was very moving. "Our house is always open to friends and we share our food." "We are rich in faith and in our church." "We are rich in our love for each other." We then asked them to gather at home every evening and talk about how rich they were. When they came back the next week, the mother was walking normally. One of the sons—a young man in his 20s—was able to tell his parents that he was gay.

I know that talking about how the poor can be rich in more important ways than material possessions is a cliché—a stereotyped phrase that has been used repeatedly over the centuries. Many people dismiss clichés because they are stereotypes, and therefore, they think they are meaningless. I believe the opposite. Certain words and phrases have become clichés precisely because they are so important. I developed most of my therapy strategies around clichés. While my colleagues were pondering the work of the French psychoanalyst, Jacques Lacan, or arguing about what school of psychoanalysis is more profound, or whether or not existential psychotherapy is worth pursuing, I was thinking about the importance of saying the essential phrases: "Please." "Thank you." "I'm sorry." "I love you." "Help me." "Please forgive me." "It was all my fault." "I'm going to protect you." "What can I do for you?" "How can I show you my love?"—and so on. Most relationship problems can be solved if people use these phrases frequently and in a heartfelt way.

As my siblings and I grew older, Gilda, our nanny still lived with us, but she wasn't expected to do anything. We had another maid, Lucy, whose only job was to take care of the room I shared with my sister, wash our hair, and take care of our clothes. One day she said to us, "I'm afraid your mother will fire me because I don't have enough work. I think she's coming to your room this morning. Please make a mess so she sees that you need me." My sister and I were delighted, and we opened our closets, threw everything on the floor and danced around stepping on the clothes. My mother came in and was horrified. She apologized to Lucy, saying we were monsters. And Lucy stayed on until she married a butler from another floor in the building.

There also was a chauffeur, Oscar. I loved him because he was so protective and patient. In the summers, we lived for three months in a beach house in Mar del Plata, a resort town about a five-hour drive from Buenos Aires. We had a cabana on the sand, and he would bring us a picnic lunch to eat on the beach, while wearing his uniform in the heat. Those summers were the happiest times growing up because I had many friends, and Oscar would drive us everywhere. One time there were so many kids that he opened the trunk and let two boys sit there.

I was the first girl to wear a bikini on that beach. I was 14 years old, and my mother had brought it from France. I put it on for the first time and went for a walk on the boardwalk. Immediately a group of boys began following me. I was amused and annoyed. From a young age, I strongly believed that everyone should be able to dress however they want to. This was fine with the American school that I attended, but it did not fit the strictly Catholic Argentine culture. Suddenly, a female police officer appeared and began walking next to me. I asked, "Why are you here? I'm not doing anything wrong. Bikinis are allowed on this beach." She said, "I know you're not doing anything wrong. I'm protecting you from those boys."

*　　*　　*

Buenos Aires looks like a concrete jungle from certain angles, but there are areas with magnificent architecture and grand French and Italian style palaces. There is a quality of faded European grandeur. It's called the Paris of South America because the city was deliberately designed to imitate Paris. There is an abundance of beautiful parks with amazing classic outdoor sculptures and fountains, elegant avenues, and a huge park with a rose garden and lake. This was the area where we lived. That's where I learned horseback riding with an English saddle. All the children of upper middle-class parents had to learn to ride, as well as to speak English or French, and to play a musical instrument.

The city is more European than Latin American, and it is famous for its restaurants and night life. As a child and adolescent, I saw little of this because I wasn't allowed to go anywhere. My friends from the American school lived in a suburb close to the school and rarely came to the city. As an older adolescent, I was allowed to go to concerts at the opera house—the Teatro Colon—with my few Argentine friends. We had a blast in the "chicken coop"—the highest floor of the theater where tickets were cheap because it was standing only. I loved the classical music performances.

As a child, I was forced to share a bedroom with my sister because my parents thought that would make us get along better. It actually led to more reasons to fight with each other! As a young adolescent, I managed to get my own room. My desk was by the window, and I spent many hours looking at a side street and at life on the block. There was a tenement house across the street that was the home of many disadvantaged people living in crowded conditions. I enjoyed observing their comings and goings. It was characteristic of the city that you could have a beautiful palace, and a few houses down, a tenement house.

When I came to the United States, I realized that many middle-class children live in the suburbs and never see poor people or bad living conditions. I believe this separation contributes to prejudice and fear of people who are different. I am grateful to have grown up in a society where poverty was visible, and where we had servants who were often kinder and wiser than some family members. This was an invaluable experience that helped me as a therapist, in working with all social classes and people from all kinds of backgrounds.

The department of psychology of the University of Buenos Aires, where I eventually became a student, was located in an old building near the port, and at night there were always drunken sailors in the streets. Many classes were in the evening, and I took the public bus to get back home and then had to walk several blocks through dark and dangerous looking streets. But I was never bothered. The city was very safe in those days.

*   *   *

My grandfather on my father's side, Leiser Madanes, ran away from Poland when he was 16 years old. His mother had died, and his father had remarried, but he did not get along with his stepmother. I seem to remember that my mother once said he was illiterate, but I don't think that was true. He probably didn't know Polish because Jews were not allowed to go to school in Poland.

But they were educated by their parents at home, so he must have been able to read and write in Yiddish. Maybe my mother was making a comparison with her Russian father who read two newspapers each day until he died in his 90s.

Leiser boarded a ship heading to America. He believed that there was only one America, and that he was going to New York, where he had relatives. He actually was headed for Buenos Aires. He was in the bowels of the ship in third class and my Russian grandmother was in first class. She belonged to a prominent Jewish family where the men were in the military, in spite of being Jewish. The men in her family realized that the revolution was coming and arranged for all the women to board a ship out of Russia. My grandmother was 16 years old. Somehow, she met Leiser on that ship. He fell in love with her and proposed marriage, but her response was, "I will not marry a Pole, especially a poor one. Get rich and then talk to me."

When he arrived in Buenos Aires, Leiser went to the city of Rosario in the province of Santa Fe, where he found work in a factory. He was an anarchist, and he organized the workers to strike so successfully that he was banned from the city for life. He returned to Buenos Aires and began to sell items door to door. But he couldn't forget my grandmother. He started a factory manufacturing raincoats and boots, and when he thought he was prosperous enough, he went to see her. "Now I'm rich. Will you marry me?" he asked. And she did. I remember that they loved each other dearly.

My grandmother, Sara, must have suffered a great deal in leaving Russia, losing everything she had and everything she knew, and having to adjust to a totally different culture without knowing the language. She had gone through all this when she was only 16 years old. Probably because of all she had been through she became somewhat harsh. She had a reputation for being a difficult person. She didn't seem to like my father, but I thought he craved her love because he even went to the extreme of learning to speak Russian so he could talk with her in her language.

My mother told me that Sara had told her that she used to cry when nursing my father because she had not wanted another baby. When my father was 12 years old, his parents sent him to live alone in a hotel in the mountains of the province of Cordoba because his asthma was severe, and the altitude was thought to be a possible cure. Later they sent him to live with an aunt because he and his brother, Manuel, quarreled constantly. In spite of all this rejection and neglect, my father adored his father and was always respectful and loving to his mother. Witnessing how my parents behaved towards their parents has been at the root of my vocation as a family therapist and continually kindles my interest in restoring love and respect towards the older generation, something so lacking in American culture.

After my grandfather died, my mother visited Sara every week and sometimes she would take me with her. Sometimes my grandmother would say critical things about my father, and my mother would respond by saying, "Mother (she always called her mother), I love you. I'm not going to fight with you no matter what you say. It takes two to fight and I'm not fighting."

Once, after we left, I asked my mother, why she didn't confront her, why she let her say bad things to her.

She answered simply, "She's your father's mother. If they fight, they will always make up because they're blood. If I quarrel with her, your father will resent it and it will be bad for my marriage." She was so right. I have told this story many times to my students and to my therapy and coaching clients.

I have some great memories of my grandmother. She used to take me out to tea, when I was probably 10 or 11 years old, without any of the other grandchildren. She would pick me up with her chauffeur and we would drive to very special tea houses that she loved. We had English tea with little sandwiches and pastries. I loved those occasions. As a family therapist, I always encourage parents and grandparents to give attention to children individually instead of always in a group.

My mother's parents were landowners in Russia. When the

pogroms started, the Cossacks attacked their home and savagely tore my grandmother's earrings from her ears. Right then, my grandfather decided to leave everything behind and get out of Russia. They had relatives who had already settled in New York, so they took a ship that was headed there. An epidemic broke out on the ship and their two children died. New York wouldn't let the passengers in because of the epidemic, so the ship went on to Buenos Aires where they knew no one. My grandfather was able to find work and eventually became a tailor. They had three more children. My mother was the youngest.

My mother's mother was named Catherine because there was a tradition in the family that the first daughter born in each generation would be named Catherine, in honor of Catherine the Great of Russia. The legend was that a great-great-great-grandfather had been the cabinet maker to the king and queen of Spain, and that Catherine, when visiting Spain, had loved his furniture and brought him and his family to Russia, saving them from the Inquisition. I was the first daughter of my generation, and I was supposed to be named Catherine, but my mother didn't like the name. She kept the "C" and called me Cloé instead for the Greek earth goddess. She read ancient mythology while she was pregnant with me and gave me the middle name Diana, for Diana the Huntress in Roman mythology.

When my grandmother, Catherine, was on her deathbed and my mother was 10 years old, she made my uncle promise that he would always take care of my mother. That is why my grandfather and uncle lived with us from the time I was 5 years old. Before that we had a very small apartment, but then we moved to a larger one that had a bedroom and bathroom upstairs separate from the rest of the home. My uncle and grandfather lived there. When we moved to the palace, they came with us.

My uncle was a bachelor, not out of choice, but because he was in love with a woman who was not Jewish. His father had told him that he would rather see him dead than married to a non-Jew. This was difficult for me to comprehend because my grandfather was a very kind man who prayed every morning and went to temple every week. He was very respectful of the servants, who were not Jewish, and of my parents who were not religious. He worked every day sewing something. My mother would make sure that he had curtains to make, clothes for us, garments to repair. She understood that he had to keep busy.

Being a bachelor suited my uncle because that way he could follow the mandate to take care of my mother, and also, as he put it, "Why buy the cow when the milk is free?" On the weekends, he went to a house that he owned in the country by the river. I assumed he was with the woman he loved. He worked for my father doing odd jobs as some sort of assistant and he took care of everything administrative that had to do with us children and with the household. As I grew older and became a teenager, he was always happy to help me with anything I wanted, even if he had to stand in line at the box office at 6:00 in the morning to get tickets for a concert I wanted to attend. To this day, I miss him. Every time I have to do anything administrative, I think, "My uncle would have done this for me." It was wonderful to grow up with a bachelor uncle who was so kind.

There was intense animosity between my father and his brothers, and there was also a strange relationship between my mother and her older sister who had raised her after their mother died. Until I was 4 or 5 years old, my mother was quite close to her sister, who often visited us. I remember those visits quite well because she had a son, three years older than me, who regularly tried to sexually molest me during them. In retrospect, I think he must have threatened me in some way and that's why I never told anyone.

When I was about 7 or 8 years old, I had an old Russian piano teacher. One day he put his hand under my sweater and fondled my non-existent breasts, then he did the same to my sister. I told my mother who was outraged and fired him immediately. Then about a year later, she hired another piano teacher who fondled my brother. He was fired too, and there were no more piano lessons, which I regret to this day. I think I couldn't tell my parents about the abuse by the school principal because it happened right after I had felt betrayed by my mother, whereas with the piano teacher, I was feeling more confident and secure in my relationship with my parents. Many years later, as a therapist, I understood the importance of discovering what had happened immediately before a traumatic event, in order to understand the reaction to the trauma.

My aunt's husband was not well educated and didn't make a good living. My mother helped to support the family. They lived a couple of blocks from us in a beautiful apartment that my parents bought for them, which overlooked the parks. Yet my mother stopped seeing my aunt and her family by the time I was about 9 years old.

I have reflected on the subject of generosity quite a bit because I am a generous person, like my father and grandfather. My mother was also very generous. She gave everything she owned to my siblings and me a long time before she died, yet my brother and sister treated her very badly. One of the problems with generosity is that it breeds resentment. Strangely, the person who receives resents the generous person because it appears that the giver is a better person based on that very generosity. And the generous person comes to resent the people who are the recipients of the generosity because it's easy to feel that they are parasites or leeches.

My aunt was an excellent cook, and my grandfather and uncle often went to Sabbath dinner at their apartment. Sometimes my siblings and I went with them. I knew that my mother considered her sister to be lower class because of the way she talked and her lack of education. My mother's brother was also lower class. But so was my mother, not in the way she spoke, but in how she laughed. I remember noticing when I was a teenager, that as soon as she laughed, anyone could figure out that she had come from a disadvantaged family background. This changed, however, when she became older. She must have trained herself to laugh differently.

My family lived with many contradictions. My paternal grandfather had been an anarchist and was an atheist who contributed hugely to building the most important Jewish temple in Buenos Aires. His wife, my Russian grandmother, was aristocratic but she respected and truly liked my mother's father, the tailor, who visited her every week after her husband died.

I was very curious about my grandfather's life in Russia. I remember several times saying to him, "Grandfather, say something to me in Russian," and he would answer, "I don't know Russian."

"Of course, you do," I would press, "you came here when you were 24 years old. You don't forget a language at that age." "The tongue is cursed," he would respond."" That's how deep his hatred of Russia was. I would persist, "Tell me something about life in Russia." "Primitive people," he would say, "in the summer they bathed naked in the river." I could never find out what river.

I often tried to get my grandfather to take my side when I had disagreements with my parents. But he never did, no matter how much I attempted to make a coalition with him against them. He would say, "I am just your grandfather, they are your parents. You have to obey your parents." In most of my books, I've written about the importance of respecting the family hierarchy. I was fortunate to learn this from my grandfather at an early age.

CHAPTER 5

No Illusions

I was 19 years old and finally studying psychology, having left Alberto to pursue his interest in economics on his own. I loved the university, even though it was hard, and the final exams were brutal. The student had to stand in front of three professors who were seated on a stage and answer any questions that they asked, while the rest of the class observed. One time I was particularly terrified. The class was Introduction to Sociology. An assistant professor came up to me as I waited my turn, and said, "I notice that you're nervous."

"Yes," I said. "I feel very intimidated by these teachers."

"Look at them," he said. "Do you think they are better people than you?"

"No," I responded. "I don't think so."

"They just know more sociology than you. That's all," he said.

His comment put things in perspective for me and I always remember his words. When I think that a student is intimidated by me, I say, "I'm not a better person than you, I just know more about psychotherapy (or coaching or whatever I'm teaching)."

Even though I loved what I was studying, I was miserable. I

was not attracted to Alberto, and he had become possessive and jealous. I was mired in existential anguish, having read all of the existential novelists that I could find. My parents' nouveau riche extravaganzas had reached new heights. My mother was obsessed with the need to marry me off before I lost my virginity, and I was obsessed with wanting to lose my virginity, not in order to be happy, but to be more miserable because it would be with a man I didn't love. This was part of my existential anguish that helped me to connect to myself and to my situation as a woman. My father was sleeping around and was delighted to have my mother so focused on me.

In my work as a family therapist, I've seen this scenario over and over again. The father, instead of intervening to ease a conflict between mother and child, is pleased that his wife is so focused on the child that she doesn't notice the father's transgressions.

However, it was not all bad. We had many good friends because Alberto was very social. We went to clubs to listen to tangos and jazz in the early evenings when the clubs were empty, and we had endless conversations about politics, literature, and philosophy. We had a couple of favorite cafes where we would sit all day trying to study, and where friends would regularly drop by and interrupt us.

I needed to leave home, but I couldn't see how I could do that and support myself. So, I gave in and agreed to marry Alberto. I was very depressed and insisted that I had to be in psychoanalysis. My father agreed to pay. My analyst had no positive effect on me. She should have told me not to get married, which is what Freud would have done, but she didn't. She was a Kleinian. In that approach the analyst doesn't give any directives. However, because I was having suicidal thoughts, she increased my sessions to five days a week. This was not unusual in those days in Buenos Aires where every psychology student who aspired to any kind of success had to be in psychoanalysis. The sessions were incredibly boring.

I told Alberto that I didn't love him and was only marrying him to get away from my parents. This didn't make him any nicer. My mother became obsessed with my trousseau—embroidered tablecloths and sheets, expensive lingerie, the wedding dress and the party—all things I didn't care about. I refused to wear a long white dress but compromised with a short one. I didn't believe in marriage. I thought it was a form of bondage. The few friends who were marrying were doing so in Uruguay because divorce was legal there. That's what I would have preferred, although not marrying at all would have been my choice.

Looking back, it's puzzling to me why I got married. I think I didn't realize the power that my mother had over me. Unconsciously I craved her love and that's why I must have obeyed her. If I had done nothing to change my situation, just stayed at home and went to school, with time my situation would have changed. Maybe I would have met someone else, or, better yet, remained single. In my work as a therapist, I've come to realize that many young people don't have a time perspective. They believe that their current situation is fixed in time and will always be the same, not realizing that everything changes with time, and most often, there is no need to take drastic action.

The wedding day arrived, and I was driving to the temple with my father in a limousine, but when we approached, somebody was waiting for us and said we should come back in half an hour. Then there was another delay, but I didn't know why. I imagined the guests must have been very restless. Later I found out that the cantor had a heart attack and died on his way to the temple. I thought to myself, "Another bad omen."

The party was at our home on the second floor of the Palacio Devoto, which still stands on Avenida Libertador in Buenos Aires, across the street from the rose gardens. Later I found out that after Alberto and I left the party, my sister had her first asthma attack. She had refused to go to the American school for high school. She went to an Argentine public school. I don't know how she finished high school, but she went to university and became a psychologist like me. I always thought she didn't like me, but I suspect she left home because she couldn't stand the way my parents treated me and how I obeyed them. She was the beautiful one and I was the smart one and we were both resentful of our assigned identities.

I wanted to go to Europe for our honeymoon, but Alberto opposed this because he didn't want my father to pay for an expensive trip. So instead, we went for a month to a remote beach in the north of Uruguay, close to the border with Brazil. The hotel was modest, but the beach was beautiful. I swam, Alberto fished, and we ate what he caught. In the evenings we played cards. When we went back to Buenos Aires people didn't recognize me because I had such a dark tan.

Back in the city, Alberto became more and more jealous and possessive. He objected to the way I dressed and frequently refused to go out with friends or to a party unless I changed my clothes. Walking down the street he would pick a fight with any man he thought was looking at me. Truthfully, I was a short, skinny young woman and there was not much to look at. One night, at a fashionable bar, he almost hit a man he thought was looking at me. I was wearing a white fur coat that covered me from my neck to my ankles. The man was probably admiring the coat. On several occasions he threatened to kill me. I remember that at least once he grabbed my neck and said, "I could kill you with one hand." I didn't think this was abuse. I thought this was normal male behavior when feeling rejected by a wife who wasn't in love. He had no clue about how to make love to a woman. But also, I was shy and didn't really know how to talk about it.

Alberto had a strange sleeping disorder. He would suddenly fall asleep no matter where he was. I remember, on more than one occasion, hosting a dinner party where he sat at the head of the table and fell asleep in front of everyone. Many years later, someone took a photograph of him, sitting at a meeting in the United Nations, sound asleep. Also, he sometimes would wake up in a rage. Once we were at the beach in Mar del Plata and he fell asleep on the sand. A little girl ran by him shouting and he jumped up flailing his arms and accidentally hit her. These were unsettling behaviors.

My mother-in-law was very intrusive. She sometimes came to my apartment while I was at the university and rearranged my closet. Sometimes she would even wash my clothes, including my underwear. I didn't know how to stop this behavior without offending her. But I developed a strategy. I started to call her at odd times and asked her when she would come to my apartment again, saying that my closet was a mess, and I could use her help. I told her I was counting on her. It took just two or three of these kind of phone calls and she stopped coming.

In spite of our difficulties, Alberto and I had some good times and good friends. It wasn't unusual for us to go to a movie at midnight, have dinner in a restaurant at 2:00 in the morning and then drive to my family's country house for the weekend. I liked the freedom of not having to be accountable to my parents, but because of Alberto's temper and jealousy, it was like jumping from the frying pan into the fire.

I became more and more depressed. I had a life size poster of Humphrey Bogart with his saddest expression—a cigarette butt hanging from his lips—by the front door of the apartment, as a reminder every time I left the house, to have no illusions. Many years later, I was invited by Rich Simon, the organizer of a major yearly psychotherapy conference, to give a keynote address. He asked me to lunch in order to discuss what I wanted to present. During the conversation, he said, "You have all these amazing strategies that you created. Do you apply them to your personal life?" I said, "No, I don't. I my personal life, I have no illusions." And I told him about the Humphrey Bogart poster. When he introduced me to the audience at the conference, he mentioned some of my work, and then he said, "Ladies and gentlemen, let me introduce you to Cloé Madanes, the woman who has no illusions." There was a piano on stage, and as I walked to the podium, he turned to the pianist and said, "Play it, Sam." And he played the theme song from *Casablanca*. It was the best, most fun introduction that I ever had as a speaker.

It was the year 2004. I started my speech with a critique of the field of psychotherapy. Here's what I said:

"Over the last 20 years, I believe that therapy has lost its way and its sense of social mission. Today, it's much harder for young therapists coming into the profession to find the role models that were available in such abundance when I started my career. One reason for this is the dominance of managed care, which took the best of brief therapy and strategic therapy and turned it into the worst possible practice. Managed-care companies took the idea that therapy could serve people better by being brief, problem focused, and practical, and used it as an opportunity to make enormous profits by bringing therapy down to its lowest possible common denominator. They reduced the number of sessions and paid so little that the more skilled, experienced therapists were driven out of practice, to be replaced by less expensive, less trained therapists who could be managed by bottom-line oriented businesspeople with no knowledge of the mental health field. With the ascendancy of managed care, much of the therapy field has become controlled by profit-driven corporations lacking any commitment to a wider vision of the public good."

"Meanwhile, the influence of psychopharmacology grew and played right into the profit-making goals of managed care. Now, even a few sessions with an unskilled therapist were no longer needed—the magic pill would solve all. The American Psychiatric Association is dominated by the pharmacological companies, which pay an average of $13,000 in gifts per year per psychiatrist to push their medications. At the recent annual meeting of the American Psychological Association, two world-renowned psychiatrists, Aaron Beck, now in his 80s and Albert Ellis, in his 90s, strongly warned psychologists not to follow the path of the psychiatrists and sell themselves to pharmacology."

"What's most inhumane about the practice of psychopharmacology today isn't just the toxic effects of the medications, but that they're typically prescribed after a 15-minute interview. It's become common practice to make enormous leaps of faith regarding the biological causes of all sorts of emotional distress, with no consideration for the underlying human relationships involved. No one takes the time to get to know the person receiving the prescription or pays attention to the social context surrounding the presenting problem. It's a shameful commentary on our clinical standards and the integrity of our scientific community that the studies showing the dangerous consequences of the use of antidepressants on children and adolescents had to come from Great Britain and Italy, not from the United States."

I still stand by these words. The state of the field has only become worse, with 5-year-old children now being labeled bipolar and prescribed medications.

*　　*　　*

When I look back at my early marriage to Alberto, I realize that I was depressed and demoralized by his behavior. It seems that I was carrying within me the oppression and abuse of women committed by men for thousands of years. I lived in a beautiful apartment overlooking a lovely park in the best neighborhood of the city. I had a live-in housekeeper. My husband was handsome and smart, and many women were attracted to him. I loved the university, even though it was unclear whether I was ever going to be able to make a living as a psychologist—the profession was not yet regulated in Argentina. I had a psychoanalyst who listened to me patiently and said very little. Yet I was trapped and miserable.

I became more and more suicidal. Then I decided that if I had a child, that would guarantee that I wouldn't kill myself. I would never abandon my own child. I talked about this in my analytic sessions, but the analyst said nothing. I got pregnant. Alberto became more possessive, jealous, and angry. I survived the pregnancy in relatively good spirits because of my friend Boris.

Boris was the son of a Russian Jew. He had gone to the elite national boys' high school, together with many of my other friends, but he never went to university, although he was a true intellectual. We were best friends and he practically lived in my house. We read the same books and talked about everything. I remember that one of the books we read was *Sexus* by Henry Miller, which was banned in Argentina, but Boris had managed to obtain a copy in English. I don't think my marriage would have survived during that time if it hadn't been for Boris. He regularly stole money and jewelry from me, but I didn't care. He worked from time to time as a bodyguard to John William Cook, a Marxist intellectual who interacted on a regular basis with Perón and Evita, and who hired him because Boris could shoot with a gun in each hand at the same time. I had to end my relationship with Boris when he falsified checks and stole a considerable amount of money from my father. To this day I miss him, even though I fully understand he didn't care for me. It was about stealing from me and from my father. But, on second thought, maybe he did care about me. Relationships are complicated and are sometimes beyond judgment.

My nanny visited me frequently and she also stole money and jewelry from me. I resented that she stole my wedding ring. That was over the top, but I still loved her.

Childbirth was more than horrific. To add to the trauma, while I was in the delivery room, my mother and Alberto smoked up my hospital room, so when the baby was finally born, I couldn't hold her and be with her until the room was ventilated and cleaned the next day. But the baby girl was healthy and beautiful. We named her Ingrid, because Alberto was in love with Ingrid Bergman. The name was fitting, given my fascination with Humphrey Bogart.

In the months that followed, I spent almost every day with the baby and Boris, like I had during the pregnancy. We would walk in the park and sometimes just sit under a tree with the baby on a blanket. People would comment about how the baby looked like Boris—blonde and round faced—and how nice it was to see a father in the park. We would just say, "Thank you."

Until the baby began to eat real food, I had never cooked anything. I didn't even know how to make coffee. On the maid's day out, if Alberto wasn't around, I would get dressed and go to a café to have breakfast. But, for the baby, I cooked the way Argentine mothers cooked in those days. When I eventually came to California and I took her—then 3-years-old—to the pediatrician for her first checkup, he asked what I fed her.

"What she likes most is filet mignon and cheese soufflé," I said.

He thought I was joking.

"I'm not," I told him. "That's what we feed young children in Argentina."

My father was in Europe with my brother when I delivered the baby. He came to see me when he got back, and he said, "I want you to understand that from now on, this is your family—your baby and your husband. I don't want you to even think about me anymore. From now on, I'm secondary in your life."

Those were wise words, but I wished he had known how miserable I was in the marriage.

During my first year with Ingrid, my brother, Claudio—who was then 17—became intensely attached to me. He would often come to my apartment to visit, and he'd stay through night, sleeping on the couch. He kept saying that I was too involved with the baby. He constantly wanted to talk with me. I realized that he was jealous and that he thought of the baby as if she were his younger sister, not his niece. Maybe this was because he was the youngest in our family and because I had been somewhat of a parental figure to him.

During the first six months, I didn't go to school, and I didn't study, But Alberto was still working and going to school. He often had friends over in the evening to study together, and I made sure that there was always dinner for everyone and a pleasant environment, while at the same time my full attention was with the baby.

One evening, Alberto said to me, "What's between you and Juan Carlos?"

"Nothing," I said, wondering what he was going to complain about now. Juan Carlos was one of his study buddies who often came to the house, but I hardly knew him.

"He asked me to meet him for coffee and he said that he was very fond of you, and that if I ever hurt you, he would kill me."

"He's only seen me with the baby," I said. "How weird!"

Many people around me reacted strangely to the birth of my child. I had a hard time setting limits with my in-laws, who wanted to show up practically every day to see the baby. Once I was nursing Ingrid in her room when the maid came in to say that my father-in-law had come to visit. I said to tell him that I would come out as soon as I finished nursing and to offer him coffee or tea while he waited. I had been studying in the living room before he came, and I had left a psychoanalytic textbook open on the coffee table. I put the baby to sleep and came into the living room. He had been reading my book. I had left it open on a somewhat shocking description of some sexual pathology.

He asked if I felt that I had to study this kind of thing because I doubted his son would be able to support me.

I explained that it was my vocation—that I wanted to be a psychologist.

His answer was simply, "I just want you to know that I will always support you if he doesn't."

Although I realized that he couldn't understand that a woman would want to have a career, I was moved by his words. He was a very good man.

Around that time, the groundbreaking book by Masters and Johnson, *Human Sexual Response*, came out. I thought that our sex life could improve, but Alberto refused to read it. I asked one of his male friends to talk to him about the book, but he still refused. Looking back, I don't understand why I didn't end the marriage then. Perhaps I thought that this was normal for women to endure.

My mother became very interested in helping me with the baby so I could continue my studies, even though I had a live-in nanny who she had picked. It didn't take long for me to realize that she was lying about being in my apartment taking care of the baby, when in fact she was spending time with a lover. I didn't blame her—she had suffered enough with my father's infidelities. In retrospect, I think that becoming a grandmother was a mid-life crisis and also a wake-up call for her.

*　*　*

I was fortunate to have excellent teachers at the university and a wealth of experiences. The students had to work with patients from the second year on until graduation—usually in five or six years. The training was equivalent to what a PsyD is in the U.S. today. One of my first experiences was at a children's hospital, talking to mothers of children who were hospitalized. Another was at a hospital near a shanty town where there was violence against and defiance of anything that appeared to be organized by the government. The psychology interns wore white coats, like the medical students, especially when going into the shanty town on home visits, because that protected us from being attacked because it identified us as doctors. I sometimes collaborated with a young Jesuit priest. I've often wondered what became of him because so many Jesuits were later tortured and killed by the military regime.

One day, during a visit, Gilda said to me, "I'm very worried about my little sister, Lili. I think she's going crazy, and she thinks so also. You're a psychology student, please help me and talk to her. She says that the Virgin Mary comes to her room and talks to her every night."

When we met, Lili confirmed that the Virgin came to her room almost every night. She stood at the foot of the bed and talked to her.

"What does she say?" I asked. "Bad things or good things?"

"All good. She talks about love and compassion and how to lead a good life."

"You're so lucky," I said. "Imagine that out of all the people in the world she chose to come to talk to you! Listen carefully and don't forget anything that she says because one of these days she will have to stop coming to you because she will have to go to someone else who needs her."

"I will," she said. "So, you don't think I'm crazy?"

"Not at all. You're just so lucky that the Virgin chose you."

Sure enough, after a few days, the Virgin stopped coming to her and Lili was fine and went about her life.

I thought, "I can do this. I can actually be a good therapist." I'm forever grateful to Lili and to my nanny for giving me confidence in my vocation. The strategy when working with delusions is simple: You don't argue about the irrational belief or experience. Instead, you redefine it in a positive way. In this case, she was not crazy, she was lucky. Then you introduce a small change or suggestion. In this case, the Virgin would soon leave to go talk to someone else. I've used this strategy, with variations, many times.

Another intervention from long ago that still stands out, emerged when I was working as a psychology intern at the children's hospital in Buenos Aires. There was a 10-year-old boy who was hospitalized for a lung condition. He was a street child. I spoke with him a couple of times and noticed that the staff was very fond of him. He was a sweet caring boy. One day I arrived at the hospital and was told that he had attempted suicide by jumping out of a window. Fortunately, he was not hurt, but the staff was very concerned and asked me to talk with him.

I said, "Hello Juan. I'm happy to see that you're well. Everyone here cares about you so much."

"Yeah," he said.

"Tell me, why did you jump out the window?"

"My mother and us," he said, "we are very poor. My mother counts on my shoeshine work to support my little brothers and sisters. I have to find her and help her."

"I understand. I think you are healthy now and will be discharged from the hospital very soon. I will get a social worker to help you get back with your mother."

He was not suicidal; he was just trying to go back to his mother to help her. Everyone had assumed this boy had wanted to kill himself, when in fact he very much wanted to live to help his mother. Nobody had actually asked him about his intentions.

I encountered many severely disturbed people at the national mental hospital where we had to do an internship. This was just before antipsychotic medications became widely used, so the patients expressed themselves sometimes in frightening ways. Professors would bring a patient to the front of the classroom and conduct humiliating interviews. One paralyzed adolescent girl was brought on stage and the professor said in front of her, "There's nothing wrong with her legs. It's a hysterical paralysis because her uncle raped her."

Once, a handsome, bearded young man was interviewed. The professor said, "Tell them who you are."

"I'm Jesus Christ," he said.

"What do you do?"

"I bring love and compassion," and he began to quote from the scriptures.

When the class ended, I was standing outside with some girls, when suddenly he was next to us.

"I'm really a carpenter," he said. "If you girls could get me a carpenter's bench, I could occupy my time."

"Yes," we said. "We'll do our best." Of course, Jesus' father was a carpenter.

We were carefully instructed about what to say and not to say to patients. One professor had an assistant among the patients, who was a paranoid schizophrenic. He told us, that as long as we didn't mention Napoleon, this patient could be fine. But if we did, he would go berserk because he thought he was Napoleon. One day the professor was giving a lecture and this patient (assistant) forgot to bring him his notes. The next day the professor had him electro-shocked. Many of the faculty were sadistic toward the patients.

But not everything was dismal. During this time, I met an architect who was quite inspiring. He had managed to gain permission to take the most disturbed male patients and organize them into a team that would build a ward on the grounds of the hospital to provide better housing for the patients. As the construction proceeded, he photographed the men on a regular basis. He put together an exhibit with the photographs and you could see the faces becoming more and more normal with hopeful, even amused expressions, in their eyes. The architect was proving that fulfilling work and connection with others, which is the best cure for mental illness. His work had a huge influence on me. I've never thought that anyone was incurable.

As shocking and traumatizing as the internships were overall, at least I was with classmates. I thought the national mental hospital was so dangerous that I wouldn't go in unless two male students walked in with me. But it was a totally different experience to have to talk to a very disturbed person one on one, especially in my own apartment.

A psychiatrist called me one day and said he had heard that I was very good at psychological testing and diagnosing and he could use some help. He was willing to pay me. I was delighted because I was still a student and didn't expect to get paid. He began to send me patients, who I saw in my apartment.

One time, a young woman (but quite a bit older than me) came in. I gave her the Rorschach test. This consists of a series of cards with ink blots. The patient is asked to look at each card and explain what they see. Pointing at a tiny dot on the second card with several even tinier dots next to it, she said, "Here is Napoleon and this is his army that he's leading into battle." This kind of response is always scored as psychotic. I was so shocked that I barely got through the other cards. I had spoken with psychotic patients before, but never in my own house. She left and I had to lie down. I thought I was going to have a heart attack. But this experience helped me to learn self-control, and I've never been this shocked again.

While I was a student, I was the teaching assistant in projective techniques. I helped the students to learn how to administer and interpret projective tests, like the Rorschach inkblot test and the Thematic Apperception Test, which are called projective because the subject's responses are not standardized and are subject to interpretation by the psychologist administering the test. As I said, in the Rorschach, the subject looks at ink spots on a card and describes what he sees. In the Thematic Apperception Test, the subject looks at pictures of people in different situations and describes what she sees. I also taught how to interpret drawings. These tests are designed to elicit unique, highly idiosyncratic responses that reflect the personality, cognitive style, and other psychological characteristics of the respondent. This experience as a teacher was invaluable in understanding the uniqueness of each individual and how any stimulus can be interpreted in myriad ways.

One of the professors was an expert in psychodrama, a therapy technique developed by Jacob Levy Moreno. It takes place in relatively large groups that could include 30 or more participants, plus several assistants who are called ego-auxiliaries, and the therapist. Typically, the therapist picks someone from the group who presents a memory of a conflict of some kind, usually with a family member. The therapist picks ego-auxiliaries to act the parts of the people involved in the conflict. The drama is played out. Then the therapist suggests modifying the scene so it will have a different outcome. The scene is played again, but now with a happier ending. This gives insight and tools to the subject in terms of how to have better relationships. I was an ego-auxiliary many times and the experience influenced the pretending and ritualistic strategies that I developed later in my career.

I was very absentminded in those days, probably because I was always thinking about what I was studying. One time, coming out of the hospital where I was doing an internship, I took a taxi, gave my address, and went into deep thought about the patient I had just seen. Suddenly I realized that the taxi had taken me way out of the city, and we were on a highway that seemed like the road to the airport. I said, "Where are you going? This isn't the way to downtown." He said, "It's a way around," and at that moment the car made a strange noise and stopped. The engine had failed. I ran out to where I could see some people standing around as if waiting for a bus. I stood with them, got on the bus, and somehow found my way home in another taxi. I don't know what the driver's intentions were, but they were not good.

Another time, I waved down a cab in the evening to go to a meeting with other students. When we got there, I opened my purse to pay, and noticed there was no meter. I said, "How much is it? You don't have a meter?" The man said, "I'm not a taxi. You should be more careful about what car you get into." I laughed, thanked him quickly, and got out in a hurry.

It was difficult to go through school during the last months of pregnancy and the first years of the baby. I mostly didn't go to class, but I kept studying all the time and was always preoccupied with my classes. Most of the professors were excellent and most of them were psychoanalysts. But there were some who came from other departments of the university and taught in the department of psychology because they couldn't teach in their own field for political reasons. For example, the professor of Anatomy and Physiology of the Nervous System was a Marxist and was not allowed to teach in the medical school. So, instead, he taught for us in the department of psychology, and the medical students who wanted to learn from the best, came to our school for his classes. This made the course very difficult because we were competing with medical students in a subject that was much more familiar to them than to us. There were also two professors of Russian psychiatry who could not teach in the medical school, and they instead taught Russian psychology in our department.

My major interest in those days was in British psychoanalysis and in authors who were interested in the childhood roots of adult pathology, such a John Bowlby and Melanie Klein. I wanted to be a psychoanalyst. Bowlby was the originator of attachment theory that emphasized the importance of constant loving care by a mother figure for a young child's healthy development. He proposed that very young children who fail to develop close emotional bonds with a caregiver will experience behavioral problems later in life.

Melanie Klein was known for her work with young children, in which observations of free play provided insights into the child's unconscious fantasy life. In early development, she found a child relates to parts rather than to complete objects, for example, the breast rather than to the mother. She called this the *paranoid-schizoid position*. The next developmental phase is the depressive position, in which the infant comes to relate to whole objects, such as the mother or father. In this phase, infants recognize the ambivalence of their feelings. The anxiety in the paranoid-schizoid position is persecutory, threatening the annihilation of the self. The child experiences hunger or pain as the breast attacking. The anxiety of the second position is depressive. In this phase, infants realize that the breast that feeds and the breast that causes pain are one and the same. Thus, children come to fear that their own destructive impulses will do harm to the loved objects.

To be studying this work while raising an infant was torture. For Bowlby, a mother should never separate from the child, even to go to a lecture, until the child is 5 years old. For Klein, infants are plagued with fear and anxiety about being attacked and about their own destructive impulses. Even though somewhere in the back of my mind I realized that these were very improbable theories, there was a part of me that felt there was some validity to them and that infants do struggle with dramatic inner conflicts.

One book that was hugely important to me was *The Divided Self,* by British psychiatrist R. D. Laing, who I would get to know personally much later in life. The book is about what causes psychosis—a psychiatric term used to refer to a disconnection from reality. Possible symptoms include delusions, hallucination, talking incoherently, and agitation. Laing argued that psychosis is the outcome of a "divided self," or the tension between the two personas within us: one, our private, authentic, real identity; and the other, the false self that we present to the world. Psychosis is a reaction to an intolerable external world that prevents us from being our authentic self.

Reading *The Divided Self*, I felt completely understood in my existential angst and my conflicts with my family. I also thought about how the book helped me to understand the plight of adolescent patients, who were the clients I wanted to work with after I finished school. I thought Laing was probably old because of his wisdom. Later, I found out that he wrote this book when he was in his 20s.

Bowlby, Melanie Klein, and R. D. Laing, all were in London at The Tavistock Institute at different times and my dream was to study there.

*   *   *

Felipe was a journalist and good friend of my parents, particularly of my mother with whom he spent many hours discussing politics. I suspected they were lovers. I liked Felipe. He was unpretentious, wrote very well, and had an analytical mind. I liked to talk with him about politics and about the state of the world.

One day, I was giving the baby a bath. She must have been around three months old when the maid knocked on the bathroom door and said that Mr. Felipe was in the living room and wanted to talk with me. I told her to explain that I was bathing the baby and would be out shortly. When I finished, I gave the baby to the maid, and I remember my arms were still wet when I went into the living room. It was strange for him to come to my apartment unannounced and I sensed this was going to be a difficult conversation.

I found him sitting on my austere blue '50s style Scandinavian couch, looking upset. He was handsome, in his early 40s, in a grey suit, dressed like a journalist.

He said, "You need to help your mother. You probably have guessed that we have had a relationship for quite a while now. She has to leave your father, with whom she's miserable, and live with me. She has to leave your father and marry me. (Divorce had just become legal.) She's afraid of doing this. You need to talk to her. She respects you and will listen to you. She values your opinion."

I said, "I can't do that. I'm the daughter, these are my parents."

Felipe continued, "Your father is a hypocrite. He doesn't care about any of you. He just wants to be wealthy and powerful. He's been cheating on your mother for years. Please, you have to do this."

I was clear, "No, I can't. He is my father. It's their decision. I can't interfere in any way."

He left. My mother stayed with my father and broke up with Felipe, but we never discussed this conversation.

I was happy that my mother had had a good sexual relationship with a man.

Meanwhile, I stayed faithful to Alberto, sort of. I say sort of because I had a platonic fling with an assistant professor of philosophy, but it never went beyond a kiss.

CHAPTER 6

Leaving Buenos Aires

In 1958, while Nixon was vice president of the United States, his motorcade was attacked in Caracas, Venezuela. This experience led Nixon to equate Latin America with violence and irrationality and to direct the United States to support dictatorial regimes in the area. In Argentina, the press reported that he was drunk during his four-day stay.

Between 1960 and 1962, the far right Tacuara Nationalist Movement was organized in Argentina. The movement engaged in several anti-Semitic bombings, particularly after Adolph Eichmann was kidnapped by the Mossad in 1960. Frondizi's government ended in 1962, yet again with intervention by the military.

On January 1, 1959, Fidel Castro drove his guerrilla army into Havana and overthrew General Fulgencio Batista, the American backed president. In April 1961, the CIA launched a full-scale invasion of Cuba. The invaders were badly outnumbered by Castro's troops and surrendered after less than 24 hours of fighting.

Many advisors to Kennedy maintained that Castro posed no real threat to America, but Kennedy believed that masterminding

Castro's removal would show Russian, Chinese, and skeptical Americans that he was serious about winning the Cold War.

In 1962, the Cuban missile crisis inflamed American-Cuban-Soviet tensions even further. On October 22, 1962, Kennedy notified Americans about the presence of nuclear armed Soviet missiles in Cuba, and he made it clear that the United States was prepared to use military force to neutralize this perceived threat to national security. Disaster was avoided when the United States agreed to Soviet leader Nikita Krushchev's offer to remove Cuban missiles in exchange for the United States promising not to invade Cuba.

On November 22, 1963, President John F. Kennedy was assassinated in Dallas, Texas, while riding in a motorcade and seated on the back of a limousine. Like so many others all over the world, I will never forget that day. I was taking a nap in my apartment in Buenos Aires. The nanny was pushing the stroller with the baby in the park. The maid knocked and opened the door of my bedroom. "I'm sorry to wake you up," she said, "but I thought you would want to know this. I just heard on the radio that President Kennedy was shot." I jumped out of bed and ran to the park, frantically looking for my baby. A few doors down the street stood a building that belonged to the Russian embassy. I thought that this might be the beginning of World War III. Nobody was safe, even in Argentina. But the soldier standing guard at the door was impassive, as usual. I found the nanny with Ingrid and went back home with a sinking feeling in my heart.

About a year later, Alberto went with our baby to visit friends who lived in an apartment two blocks away. Minutes after they left, the building collapsed in an explosion. Apparently, there were terrorists manufacturing bombs in one of the apartments and something had gone wrong. I was filled with dread and with fear that this was a sample of what was to come.

On April 28, 1965, 42,000 American troops invaded the Dominican Republic. By the end of the invasion, more than 3,000 Dominicans and 31 American servicemen had lost their lives. In

1963, Bosch—the head of the Dominican Revolutionary Party and a leading writer and intellectual—had won the first free presidential election in 30 years. But his pro-Castro sentiments and the uneasiness he inspired in business sectors fueled a military coup seven months later that installed a three-man military junta. President Lyndon Johnson sent U.S. Marines to the island to support the junta and to place Joaquin Balaguer back in power. Balaguer had succeeded General Rafael Trujillo, the brutal dictator who ruled the country with Washington's blessing for 31 years. Trujillo used the U.S. trained National Guard to banish, torture, or kill his opponents.

By the end of April 1965, I was close to graduating as a *licenciada* in psychology. I went to the university to hand in a paper, and in the main lobby, hanging from the very high ceiling, was a huge replica of a U.S. Marine coming down attached to a parachute and holding a machine gun. I was stopped: "We need you to give blood for our comrades in the Dominican Republic."

"I'm sorry," I said, "I'm too thin. Doctor's orders." I was too thin and had been very sickly. I felt this was the beginning of worse things to come.

By 1965, when the Dominican invasion reversed the United States adherence to its pledge to foreswear unilateral military intervention, the U.S. had asserted its sphere of influence throughout the whole Western Hemisphere. In what amounted to an after-the-fact defense of the Dominican intervention, the United States House of Representatives declared that even the threat of intervention by "the subversive forces known as international communism" would justify the U.S. resorting to armed force, in the "exercise of individual self-defense." This attitude held that the U.S. government had a right to remove whatever forces it deemed threatening, and it was this presupposition that conditioned the Nixon-Kissinger response to Salvador Allende's election in Chile.

In Argentina, new elections were held in 1963, and neither Peronists nor Communists were allowed to participate. Arturo Illia, a moderate, won the elections and outlawed the Tacuara terrorist organization in 1965. Illia was eventually ousted in another military coup in 1966. By then I was already in Berkeley, California.

*   *   *

From a very young age, my favorite games involved acting and pretending. I loved pirate novels and read all of Emilio Salgari. Another favorite was *The Three Musketeers*. The movies I loved best were about pirates, especially the Errol Flynn movies. Weekends at the country club and the summers at the beach are among my fondest memories because there were many children for me to play with and we were outside all the time. I organized my friends to reenact a movie I had seen or a book I had read. I was usually the princess, and my sister acted the part of the lady-in-waiting. Sometimes I was the pirate or the knight in shining armor. We used props and created scenarios with ships, horses, and swords.

This interest in the theatrical resurfaced when I became a therapist. One of my contributions to the field, is the strategy of pretending that I described in my book, *Strategic Family Therapy*. Often children develop problem behaviors when they discover that these behaviors can distract parents from other, perhaps more serious issues. For example, a child may have painful headaches that require parental attention, so the parents will focus on the child and not on their own issues. The therapist can ask the child to pretend to have a headache and the parents to do whatever they do for the real headache, but to do it for the pretend headache. In this way, the child doesn't have to have the real headache to be helpful to the parents. The pretend headache will do. But the parents' helpfulness is also a pretense, and the whole interaction turns into a game.

By the same token, a depressed spouse can pretend to be depressed and the other spouse can pretend to help. The idea is that if you are pretending to be depressed, you can't really be depressed, because then you aren't pretending. I have taught this strategy for many years to many generations of therapists.

Another one of my contributions is my "repentance and apology strategy," which consists of a ritualistic series of steps to be used when there is violence in the family. I developed this strategy through my work with juvenile sex offenders. The whole family gathers, and after a discussion of the spiritual pain inflicted by the abuser, the offender gets on his knees and expresses his sorrow and repentance to the victim for what he did. The family decides whether the offender is sincere in his repentance, and if he's not, he has to apologize over and over again until everyone agrees that he's sincere.

I spent most of my career teaching family therapy from behind a one-way mirror. On one side of the glass, a student works with a family or a couple. On the other side, I (the supervisor) sit with a group of students who are observing the therapy. I call the therapist with instructions over the phone, or the therapist comes out of the room to discuss with me how to proceed. There is also a camera that films the therapy. The group of students sits behind the one-way mirror watching the drama unfold on the other side of the glass. Sometimes they watch the action on a television screen that reproduces with close-ups and at different angles the view from behind the mirror. The supervisor is the drama's director, organizing the action on both sides of the screen and arranging simultaneously the solution to the client's problems and the education and entertainment of the students. Education today must include a component of entertainment.

As an adolescent and young adult, I was greatly influenced by my father's cousin, Cecilio Madanes, who was a leading figure in Argentine theater since 1950 when he came back from studying with Louis Jouvet in Paris. In 1957, he created "Teatro Caminito," an extraordinary street theater experience in the picturesque Italian neighborhood of La Boca in Buenos Aires. It lasted until 1973. The theater featured the works of Shakespeare, Molière, and Garcia Lorca, among others and enlisted the participation of leading Argentine actors. Cecilio also directed several plays in national theaters, including *Dangerous Relationships* and *Equus*. Between 1983 and 1986, he was director of the opera house, Teatro Colon, which is on a par with the opera of Milan and the Paris Opera.

Cecilio was often at my house and had always been best friends with my parents. He had been very ill as a child, and as a result, had a bad leg and walked with a cane. My father supported him financially during his studies in Paris. When my father became the director of the national television channel, he gave Cecilio a job. It was with him that my parents went to Paris to buy the outrageous decor that they brought back to our house, and that's why our house looked more like the set of a French or Italian opera than like a home. As an adolescent, Cecilio always took my side and helped me with my parents. I remember that he talked my father into letting me wear high heels, which was very important to me.

A huge disappointment was that, when we were in exile, Cecilio turned against my father. He wrote a letter complaining that he couldn't get a job because he had the same last name—Madanes. The tone of the letter was negative and resentful, as though he had forgotten all that my father had done for him during the eight years that he lived in Paris and for many years after that. I learned at an early age that the response to generosity is often resentment, especially from those whom one holds dear.

I remember one time, after I was married, I was throwing a dinner party. My father asked me who was coming. I named the guests and he asked why I didn't invite Cecilio, to which I replied, "Because he's an ungrateful hypocrite who turned against you. Remember?"

My father responded matter-of-factly, "That doesn't matter, he's entertaining. That's what matters at a dinner party."

I liked that way of thinking, but I still didn't invite him. Eventually he reconciled with my parents, and all was forgiven.

Many years later, Cecilio came to a workshop I was giving in

New York. I showed a video where I was directing family members on what to say to each other and what emotion to experience. I've always been very directive in my therapies. Afterward, Cecilio said, "Girl, you're in my line of work. What you teach is theater."

He was gay but always in the closet. It was shortly before he died that he extended the invitation: "I want you to meet my friend." I finally met his partner of many years in the beautiful house full of amazing art where they lived.

In 1965, the year that I graduated from the university, Buenos Aires was a truly cosmopolitan city with a booming arts and literature scene. The 1965 season was brimming with life: a lavish presentation of Boris Goudonov, the renowned Comedie Francaise, along with Brecht, Albee, Ionesco and Garcia Lorca. The art theaters showed the latest films by Bergman, Truffaut, and Antonioni, and the countless bookstores displayed writings by Simone de Beauvoir and Georg Lukacs. Jorge Luis Borges was regularly featured in the literary magazine *Sur* and in the newspaper *La Nación*.

The lifestyle in my social class was glamorous and fun. Bars and restaurants were open until dawn. Vacations were at least one month-long in beach houses in Punta del Este, Uruguay. We were always surrounded by friends and conversations were always interesting. Lawyers took the month of January off (the seasons are reversed in South America) and psychoanalysts (I belonged to this group) took the month of February. But most of the time we vacationed for two months.

The department of psychology at the University of Buenos Aires was also booming, and the professors were interesting, dedicated, and taught at the highest level. The last class that I took was Advanced Clinical Psychology, which included communication theory and the work of Gregory Bateson and his group. The Bateson Project (1953-1963) was the name given to a groundbreaking collaboration organized by Gregory Bateson. This collaboration was responsible for some of the most important papers and innovations in communication and psychotherapy in the 1950s and early 1960s. The other members were Don Jackson, Jay Haley, and John Weakland. The group proposed the double-bind theory of schizophrenia in the seminal paper: "Toward a Theory of Schizophrenia."

The cause of schizophrenia is still not known. It's a diagnosis usually applied to people who seem out of touch with reality and whose speech or behavior appears disorganized. These people may also experience difficulty with concentration and memory, and hear voices as well as have hallucinations and delusions.

The Bateson group described the characteristics of a double-bind relationship and proposed that an ongoing relationship with these characteristics would lead to schizophrenic behavior.

a) When the subject is involved in an intense relationship—that is, a relationship in which he feels it is vitally important—that he discriminate accurately what sort of message is being communicated so that he may respond appropriately.

b) And the subject is caught in a situation in which the other person is expressing two orders of message and one of these denies the other.

c) And the subject is unable to comment on the messages being expressed to correct his discrimination of what order of message to respond to, i.e., he cannot make a meta-communicative statement.

d) And the subject cannot leave the relationship, i.e., a child dependent on the parents.

The double-bind theory was originally formulated to explain what happens to a child growing up in a situation where he is frequently given double-bind messages, but it applies to many other social contexts. This was precisely the problem in the legal circles of the United States prior to the Fifth Amendment to the U.S. Constitution being applied to state action. A person could be subpoenaed to testify in a federal case and given Fifth Amendment immunity for testimony in that case. However, since the immunity did not apply to a state prosecution, the person could refuse to testify at the federal level, despite being given immunity thus subjecting the person to imprisonment for contempt of court. Or the person could testify, and the information being coerced in the federal proceeding could then be used to convict the person in a state proceeding.

The Bateson group proposed that growing up amidst perpetual double binds could lead to learned patterns of confusion in thinking and communication. When I studied the Bateson Project, I began to change my mind about studying in London. I realized that psychoanalysis, with its focus on the intra psychic, was becoming a thing of the past and the future lay in understanding communication between real people, not just communication going on inside a person's head. For my last exam before graduating, I was alone in a classroom with Carlos Sluzki, a psychiatrist who was assistant to the professor teaching the course. He said, "Write about theories of schizophrenia." I wrote and wrote and wrote.

After about an hour he announced, "When are you going to stop? I don't have all day you know. I don't know about you, but I have a life."

"I can't stop now," I said. "I'm writing about the Bateson Project."

"They are at the Mental Research Institute in Palo Alto, California," he said. "I'm thinking of going there."

I said, "I'm going there too."

And that same year I was there. He came later. We are good friends to this day.

*   *   *

During his last year studying economics in Buenos Aires, Alberto obtained a scholarship from the Ford Foundation to come to the United States for a PhD program. I wasn't happy about this because I still had dreams of going to London for a doctorate myself. But I understood that this was a very special opportunity with all expenses paid. Alberto promised that after he got his PhD, we would go to London for mine. An important issue for us was where in the United States we would be willing to live. We agreed that we would refuse to go to the South because of the prevalent racism. I didn't want to go where the winters were long and extremely cold. Alberto explained this to the foundation, and they accepted that we could go to the University of California at Berkeley, where Alberto could pursue a PhD in agricultural economics, which was his interest.

When I told my father, he said, "I'm not letting you go without a nanny to help with the child. American women are slaves, tied to the household and not able to study or do anything that interests them. You can only go with a nanny, and I'll pay for her."

Even though I was an adult and married, my father still had a great deal of authority over me. I told Alberto that I would only go with a nanny and that he would have to explain this to the people at the foundation so they would give her a visa. Even though this was unheard of, they gave the nanny the visa and we arrived in Berkeley in August 1965.

The scholarship was not only for Alberto. There was a small group of Argentinians who were recruited for this program and placed at different universities all over the United States. They were all married men and most of them had children. I was the only professional woman among the wives. There was an introductory seminar in Minneapolis and from there we drove all the way to Berkeley.

The foundation had arranged for us to have student housing in Berkeley, but Alberto didn't even want to show me the apartment. He told them that we would rent our own house and would pay for it. Actually, my father paid for it. But it was extremely difficult to find someone who would rent to us and finally one landlady told me that she thought we were a threesome and that we were lying when we said the other young woman was a nanny. I explained in detail about how people in Argentina employed nannies, about my father not letting me come without one, and about him paying the rent. Finally, she agreed to rent to us. It was a very small house in a working-class neighborhood near the university.

CHAPTER 7

Berkeley

We arrived in Berkeley at the time of the Berkeley protests or Berkeley revolution. Many of these protests were part of the Free Speech Movement that was fighting to obtain the right to political activism within the university. Both were related to the massive protests against the Vietnam War. The Black Panther Party, founded in 1966, aimed to improve civil rights of African Americans and to end police brutality. All these activities were intertwined, and we quickly made friends with activists in all of the groups. On October 15, 1965, Alberto took our daughter to the March down Telegraph Avenue against the Vietnam War.

One of my first experiences at Berkeley was visiting Sproul Hall where the student union was located. I started a conversation with a student and when I told him that I had graduated from the University of Buenos Aires, it turned out that he knew all about the university. He told me that much of the activism in Berkeley was modeled after the accomplishments of the University of Buenos Aires' students. I felt very proud.

In Buenos Aires, not only was there politics within the university in the sense of elections of student representatives to governing boards, but students also stood in the Latin American tradition of intense student interest in national politics. Voting is compulsory in Argentina on penalty of a fine and the legal voting age is 18. At the University of Buenos Aires, tuition is free for all students, regardless of their financial status and academic achievements. It was only in 1958 that legislation authorized the establishment of private universities amid intense protests by students at the University of Buenos Aires.

By the time I graduated as '*Licenciada en Psicologia*,' it was too late to apply to graduate school in Berkeley. But I was allowed to audit two classes in clinical psychology. There were just a few students in each class. They were very competitive with each other and not friendly. It was a cut-throat environment, especially in contrast to the camaraderie and enthusiasm at the University of Buenos Aires, where we didn't care for the treatment of knowledge as property. We lent our notes to each other and shared our insights. At Berkeley, the students were mostly not a happy lot. I was constantly harassed by the professors with sexual innuendoes. I could not adjust to the possessive individualism of an American graduate school. In Argentina, we studied together often through the night. We shared our notes and our insights. After just a few months, I made the second biggest mistake in my career (the first was not going to Radcliffe).

When the classes that I audited ended, the chairman of the department called me to his office and said, "Okay, you're in."

"In what?" I asked.

"In the PhD program. We would like to have you in our PhD program."

I said, "But I didn't apply."

"I know," he said, "but we would like to have you in the program."

I said, "No, thank you. This is a very stressful atmosphere. I have a young daughter and I don't want her to feel that I'm going through so much stress."

He asked if the professors were harassing me.

"No, no," I lied. I didn't want to accuse anyone.

My life would have been so much easier if I had gotten the PhD. Eventually, I got an honorary doctorate from the University of San Francisco, but that was many years later.

I made some good friends in Berkeley. One was a psychologist named Ruth. One day, for some reason, I told her that I was Jewish. She advised me, "When people ask you where you're from, don't say, 'I'm Argentine.' Say, 'I'm Jewish Argentine.' Being Jewish raises your IQ by 30 points immediately." This was a shock to me. Being Jewish in Argentina was always detrimental. Here it made you more valuable. I had not realized before how much I took Argentina anti-Semitism for granted. It was like being a slave, but not knowing you're a slave until you become free. It's hard to recognize prejudice when it's all that you've known.

Berkeley was a wild place, but I was a very serious student, and I didn't even smoke pot once, or try acid. I was invited to crazy parties, and I never went. There were rumors of orgies and nude encounter groups. Then there was a huge venereal disease epidemic and one of my friends almost died. The hippies seemed fun at first, but I soon realized that they were as self-righteous as if they had been religious fundamentalists, insisting on pushing their counterculture as the only way to live and promoting a fake spirituality. But those were really sad times when almost everyone I knew had a relative or a friend who was a soldier in Vietnam or who had died there. Many young men were going to Canada to escape the draft.

I was very depressed during the first few months in Berkeley—the news about the Vietnam War, the strange environment, the bad relationship with my husband. I had trouble coping with all this. What was most puzzling was the war in Vietnam. A professor of psychoanalysis in Buenos Aires, Luis Rascovsky, had written a book titled *Filicide*. He proposed that Freud was mistaken. In his description of the Oedipus Complex, Freud had proposed that unconsciously every son wants to kill his father in order to have sex with his mother. According to Rascovsky, it's the father who wants to kill his son, not the other way around. The proof is that all wars are fought by young men whose fathers put them in harm's way and send them to die. In my view, this was precisely what was happening with the Vietnam War.

I was fortunate to meet and make friends with very special people in Berkeley. One was Margaret Singer, a psychologist who had made important contributions to the field of communication and to psychological testing. I became her assistant and spent many days working at her house analyzing data. Through her I met Lyman Wynne, her associate, and became his assistant. At the time, he was also spending a sabbatical at Stanford University. I learned a great deal from both of them, professionally and in my personal life. Lyman had volunteered for an LSD experiment at Stanford. He told me to never take acid. He had such a psychotic experience that he thought he would never come back to reality.

In 1968, when Martin Luther King and Robert Kennedy were assassinated, it didn't seem like the United States was a viable country to live in. Hatred and racism were sinister and pervasive.

The Mental Research Institute, where the Bateson Project had developed, was an hour's drive from Berkeley. I showed up one day, unannounced, and said, "I'm an Argentine psychologist and I want to work for free as a research assistant to anybody here who needs an assistant."

Paul Watzlawick, one of the research associates at the institute said that he needed an assistant and I worked for him for almost three years.

The Mental Research Institute (MRI) was founded by Don D. Jackson and colleagues in 1958. By the time I got there in 1965 it had become established as a center of interactional/systemic studies, psychotherapy, and family therapy. It became the go-to place for any therapist who wanted to be on the cutting edge of psychotherapy research and practice. Fostering a climate of almost pure experimentalism, MRI started the first formal training in family therapy, produced some of the seminal early papers and books in the field, and became a place where some of the field's leading figures came to work or just hang out. When I was there, Virginia Satir had just left after running the family therapy training program. Don Jackson was the director. Jay Haley, John Weakland, and Richard Fisch were there. The focus of MRI was to explore the use of an interactional approach to better understand and more effectively resolve human problems from the family to all other levels of social organization. This was exactly what interested me, and I was very excited to be there.

Paul Watzlawick was an Austrian-American family therapist, communication theorist, and philosopher. He believed that people create their own suffering in the very act of trying to fix their emotional problems. When I started working for him, he was writing his most influential book, *Pragmatics of Human Communication*, together with Don Jackson and Janet Beavin. I helped him with scoring some data and doing research for his book. He was an old-fashioned gentleman and a pleasure to work with. Paul was an important influence in my work, in the sense that he was very good at explaining how a problem was created and why it persisted; but he was not so good at explaining how to solve the problem in therapy. He did not address issues of hierarchy within a system, which was an important part of the contribution I would make years later. Eventually, when I was a teacher in my own right, and we were participating in the same conferences, he would come to hear me and stand in the back of the room. I loved to watch him cracking up with laughter at the outrageous stories I told about the way I do therapy.

Don Jackson was a psychiatrist best known for his pioneering work in family therapy. He worked with Bateson, Haley, and Weakland in developing the double-bind theory of schizophrenia and he established the discipline of family therapy at the Mental Research Institute. I observed him working with families from behind a one-way mirror many times. When he died in 1968 from an overdose of pain killers at the age of 48, all of us at the MRI were in shock and grief. There were rumors that he had committed suicide, though this didn't make sense to me. He was in the process of divorcing his wife and he was involved with another woman and that was part of what fueled those rumors. He had suffered from severe back pain for years and injected himself with pain killers. The overdose was an accident. His death was a great loss. I volunteered to finish his research on families with children suffering from ulcerative colitis and published two papers on the subject.

Jay Haley was one of the founding figures of brief and family therapy and of the strategic model of psychotherapy. He had a masters' degree in communication from Stanford University, where he met the anthropologist, Gregory Bateson, who invited him to join a communications research project that became known as the Bateson Project. That was one of the driving factors in the creation of family therapy. He joined MRI when Don Jackson founded it in 1958. I read his book, *Strategies of Psychotherapy*, when I was a student in Argentina. At the time, I was very psychoanalytical in my thinking and going through psychoanalysis myself. The book is mainly a critique of psychoanalysis and it infuriated me because I felt the criticism was unfair and unjustified. During all the time that I was at the MRI, I refused to meet Jay because I was so insulted by that book. If I was in a meeting and he would walk in, I would walk out. If I was discussing a topic with someone and they suggested we go to Jay's office to check in with him, I would refuse, making it clear I wasn't interested in Jay's opinions. Little did I know that I would end up marrying him.

John Weakland was a chemical engineer when he met anthropologist, Gregory Bateson, and decided to work with him on his research on schizophrenia and alcoholism at the Veterans Hospital in Palo Alto. He helped create the Brief Therapy Center at the MRI and wrote numerous books on therapy strategies. He was always joking and was much loved by everyone.

Janet Beavin was my age. She was working with Paul Watzlawick and Don Jackson on their book, *Pragmatics of Human Communication*. We were the same age and became good friends and had many good times together. One day we were discussing something at the MRI, and she said, "Let's ask John what he thinks."

I demurred, explaining I was tired of his sexual innuendos. She assured me that he was harmless and had a heart condition to boot.

She thought it was silly to miss out on interacting with someone so smart because he was flirtatious. She had an idea and made me promise to follow her lead.

I reluctantly agreed. I was wearing a fitted mini dress with a wide brown leather belt, which was fashionable at the time. We went into John's office and Janet said, "Hello John, Cloé and I were just discussing one of your papers and we have a question."

Right on cue, he responded, "I don't know that I can focus on your question. Looking at Cloé, with that sexy dress and that belt … it's too distracting."

Janet ran with it, and she came to stand behind me. "I'm going to unzip her dress so she won't be wearing it anymore and we can get past this."

"No," said John, putting his hand over his heart, "please don't. I have a heart condition."

I was laughing. "Well, then stop bothering her all the time and answer our questions," said Janet smiling. We sat down and had an interesting conversation with John, who never bothered me again.

*　*　*

When I met Aaron, he was a professor of psychology at a local university and he was dating a friend of mine, Julie. I liked him right away. So did Alberto, and the four of us often spent time together. I frequently had them over for dinner. He was an interesting man, with a great sense of humor and I learned a great deal from him. He loved to talk with my young daughter, who tried to teach him to speak Spanish.

One evening, he and Julie came to my house, and he had just bought a new sports car. It was beautiful and I said so. He asked if I wanted to drive it, and a bit surprised, I happily accepted the invitation. It had room for only two, so we left Alberto and Julie behind.

After a few minutes on the road, Aaron asked me to stop the car for a few minutes because he had something to say.

He said something to the effect that he really cared about me, that he knew I was unhappy in my marriage, that he wanted to be with me. I was shocked, and immediately protested, reminding him that Julie was my friend. He pressed on, explaining that he and Julie were not serious, and he knew I would be happy with him.

I was clear: "I'm married, and I have a daughter, and Julie is my friend. This conversation never happened."

We went back to the house. I really liked Aaron and I was attracted to him, but I thought, "He's just another one of these American professors who doesn't know how to behave with a woman." We saw less of Aaron and Julie after that day. Eventually, they got married and moved out of state.

About 25 years later, I ran into Julie at a conference. She said, "You probably don't know that Aaron died."

I had not known.

Her next words came as a shock: "He killed himself. Shot himself in the head in his office, making sure that I could be the one to find him. I think you might want to know that there was no suicide note, just an old piece of paper with your handwriting. You had translated a poem from Spanish for him."

I was deeply saddened. To this day I wonder, what if I had taken his words seriously, what if I had chosen a different path. Why had he kept this poem for so many years and why did he die looking at it? Maybe he actually loved me. How would my life had been different if that day in his car I had said, "Yes, let's go off together and be happy." I've always had the desire to live a life totally different from my own. I've always had the secret desire to totally step out of my context and my obligations. I had the opportunity that evening in Berkeley. I didn't take it.

*   *   *

At the same time that I was working at the Mental Research Institute, I was a student at the Center for Training in Community Psychiatry in Berkeley. The center was created by Portia Bell Hume, MD, and Janmeja "Meji" Singh, PhD. Portia Bell Hume was a pioneer in developing community mental health and was instrumental in the writing and passage of California's Short-Doyle Act in 1957, also known as the Community Mental Health Services Act. This act sought to encourage the treatment of patients suffering from a psychiatric disorder in their home community, with the assistance of local medical resources, instead of placing them far from home and family.

The emphasis of the training was on preventive psychiatry. We learned how to work as consultants to other professionals, such as nurses, teachers, doctors, and community leaders, in order to prevent psychiatric disorders and institutionalizations. The training was excellent. It was based on Gerald Caplan's work in Israel, and it opened a whole different way of thinking for me. I became very good friends with Meji, who was a great teacher. Portia was a great role model as a female leader.

The schools in Berkeley were integrated in 1968. The department of clinical psychology offered to send consultants to a school in Berkeley to help the teachers with any challenges they might have. I was asked to participate because of my involvement with the department and my interest in community work. I realized this was a historic moment in the United States and was delighted to help.

A fourth-grade teacher approached me one day at the school. She said she wanted to discuss a problem with a girl in her classroom, Ann, who was African American, and this was her first year in the school. The teacher was a beautiful black, young woman. She said that Ann was very shy—a small child who was disliked by the other children who pestered her constantly. They had gotten to the point that three girls had thrown stones at her when she was walking home from school. The teacher had referred Ann for testing but done nothing about the three girls. From her choice of words and her tone of voice I realized that she didn't like Ann. This teacher was well known in the school for being able to control the most difficult, aggressive boys. I realized that Ann represented to the teacher the part of herself that she dreaded to be—a timid girl who didn't stand up for herself. She told me, without any sign of compassion, that Ann often spent time in class writing letters to her father, who had abandoned the family and gone back to Africa.

When I asked about Ann's friends, it turned out that she had one best friend—a tall girl who was the brightest girl in the class. I pointed out to the teacher that research shows that the best predictor of a child's intelligence is who her friends are, so most probably Ann was also very intelligent, but it didn't show because of her shyness. The teacher was interested in this idea. I said, "I don't know how to solve this. I'm not a teacher. I think maybe if she could be chosen for something special in relation to the other students, maybe something like that could help. But I don't know what educational tools could be used for that."

The teacher said that she would think about it. A couple of weeks later, she told me that she had spent two weeks after school preparing a special presentation with Ann. It was a slide presentation and she wanted Ann to do the narration. But knowing that standing in front of the class would be too difficult for her, she patiently recorded Ann's narration, and played the performance to the class. The presentation was very successful and now the children liked Ann and even admired her.

I'll never forget that little girl and that teacher because they both represented parts of me that I also struggled with—the ambitious, strong woman, and the timid little girl. Most people have problems empathizing with those who represent the weaker aspects of themselves. Ann represented the weaker aspect of the teacher, but as soon as she saw that Ann's strength might be her intelligence, she was able to feel empathy for her and she figured out how to help her.

*　　*　　*

My father came to visit us in Berkeley. I had to go to a class on the first day he was there so I gave him my car and suggested that he go to San Francisco to the Haight-Ashbury district where he could walk around, look at the hippies, and have a good time.

He came back with a flower painted on his cheek, and he said to me, "You study too hard. You should love more and work less. You need to have more fun." He had been totally seduced by the hippie scene.

I was friends with a psychiatrist who was taking the training in community mental health, and I asked him if he had any suggestions for where to take my father in San Francisco. He said he would give me his key to the Playboy Club. We went there—my father, Alberto, and me. As soon as we entered, there were bunny girls all over the place. It was a mansion with different shows and activities going on in various rooms. We decided to see a comedy routine. We sat down at a small round table and the lights went off. When they came on again, the headlights were shining on the three of us, and the two comedians were talking about us: "Look at that girl in the psychedelic dress (that was me), she's with her sugar daddy and her gigolo," and on and on. My father whispered, "Don't say anything." And we didn't. Even though it was embarrassing we had a blast.

One time my father and I went to San Francisco because he wanted to buy me some nice clothes at one of the fancy department stores. We went to Joseph Magnin—an upscale store that mostly catered to young women. I tried on clothes and showed them to him, and he helped me pick. At one point, the saleswoman came into the dressing room and said to me, "You call him Papa, but he is really your Papa, isn't he?" "Of course," I said. "He's my father. He came to visit from Argentina." It seemed we drew attention to ourselves wherever we went.

CHAPTER 8

The Queen Elizabeth

June 1966, Argentina. A coup established General Juan Carlos Ongania as the de facto president, supported by several labor leaders. Ongania aimed at establishing a new political and social order, opposed both to liberal democracy and to communism. Political scientist, Guillermo O'Donnell, named this type of regime "authoritarian-bureaucratic state," similar to the Brazilian military regime at the time and to Pinochet's regime, which started later in Chile.

Ongania implemented a series of extreme right-wing policies, such as suspending collective labor conventions and ending the right to strike. He was responsible for the "The Night of the Long Truncheons". It was July 1966. The police were ordered to invade the Faculty of Sciences of the University of Buenos Aires. They beat up and arrested students and professors. The university repression led to the exile of 301 university professors.

Ongania also ordered repression with all regard to all forms of "immoralism," defined as miniskirts, long hair for young men, and all avant-garde artistic movements. This "morality campaign" alienated the middle classes, who made up much of the universities. Ongania banned all political parties, and he jailed politicians and labor leaders, closed Congress, and even dismissed members of the Supreme Court.

Peronists continued to resist with increasing violence and began to create guerrilla organizations. Censorship was harsh. A satirical magazine was shut down. An Argentine opera was banned. Even the Instituto Di Tella, the most famous avant-garde cultural center in Latin America, was closed. The director at the time was Torcuato Di Tella, the professor who had helped me overcome my fear of oral exams during my first year studying psychology. He left the country and came to Berkeley where we became good friends. However, in spite of all the censorship, Argentine writers, such as Borges, Bioy Casares, Cortazar, Sábato, and Puig continued to produce tirelessly.

During the 1960s, the Montoneros were a left-wing Peronist group known for violent urban terrorist actions, such as political kidnappings and assassinations. Primarily composed of young men and women of the middle class, the Montoneros were dedicated to overthrowing the government. They funded themselves through bank robberies and with the large ransoms paid to them for the release of their kidnap victims.

Another terrorist left-wing group was the People's Revolutionary Army (Ejército Revolucionario del Pueblo—ERP). They launched a guerrilla campaign against Ongania's dictatorship in 1969, using assassinations and kidnappings of government officials and foreign company executives. Allegedly, they occupied 52 towns, robbed 166 banks, and took $76 million in ransoms for the kidnappings of 185 people.

*   *   *

In spite of the military dictatorship and the terrorist activity, we went back to Buenos Aires. I had decided to have another child and I didn't want to have a baby in a hospital in the United States, away from my family. Alberto had finished his course work and planned to write his dissertation for the PhD in agricultural economics in Argentina. He never finished it. It was clear to me that I would never get to fulfill my dream of studying in London.

My daughter, Magali, was born on November 28, 1969, at dawn on the day after the last Beatles concert together. I refused to go to the hospital until the concert was over and I barely made it. I wanted to call her Samantha, but the name was not allowed in Argentina. Because it's a Catholic country, one could only name a child after a saint. I fought this in court, but I lost. I saw that the name Magali was permitted, even though it's not the name of a saint, and I chose it. It's a beautiful name, popular in the south of France and in Italy.

We still had our apartment, but after the baby was born, we spent the summer in a rented house in the suburbs because I felt Magali was too young to take her to Punta del Este where my family always vacationed. The nanny came back to Argentina with us to visit her family, and then went back to Berkeley to marry an engineer. She was now fluent in English and very American. Soon we sold our apartment and moved to a house in the suburbs.

I started to work part-time for free at a public hospital near my house that served a low-income population. It was a tradition in Argentina that every doctor and psychologist worked several mornings *pro bono* at public hospitals. I did family therapy with very disturbed people, and sometimes I went to their homes if the adolescent or adult child refused to come to see me. I noticed that my colleagues were cold to me, and I could hardly engage them in conversation. One day, I was hanging out with an old friend from the university, and I told her that people were quite cold to me, and I wondered if she had any idea why.

She said without hesitation, "Everybody thinks you work for the CIA."

She went on, "They think that's why you're interested in working with the poor and you visit their homes because you report to the CIA about where the shanty towns are and where could be a breeding ground for terrorists."

The next time there was a meeting of the whole staff I had something to say: "I want everyone to know that I don't work for the CIA. Think for a moment—I have two little girls. Would I be putting them in danger? I belong to a wealthy family. Why would I put myself in danger? For what? What could the CIA pay me that would make it worth my while? I like working with the poor because I like helping the disadvantaged. That's all."

They were nicer to me after that.

I received a call from the director of the national mental hospital. He had heard that I was back from working at the Mental Research Institute and wanted like to invite me to train the psychiatric residents in family therapy. I happily accepted. I was going to work there one day a week. I explained that I like to do a very practical training. So instead of lecturing to them, I would like them to prepare some cases for discussion, starting on the first day of training. My teaching would always be based on discussions of cases that they were actually working with.

I arrived at the same hospital where I had done an internship. I went into a large room of approximately 30 psychiatric residents—all men. Turns out, this was the first time that they were going to be taught by a woman—and by a psychologist, not a psychiatrist. Also, they were all about my age or older than me.

I introduced myself and asked if anyone had a case that they would like to discuss. Three of them stood up and said they had prepared a case of an adolescent girl who was diagnosed schizophrenic and was thought disordered and delusional. They thought that this was an especially appropriate case for training in family therapy because the girl's father was very interested in her and visited her frequently. They actually had a recording of the father talking about the girl.

I suggested we listen to it.

They turned it on and there was the voice of the father talking about what a moral person he was, how his values were so important to him, how he wanted his daughter to live by the highest values, and how morality is the most important thing in life. He was obviously holier-than-thou and most probably hiding something horrible. After about five minutes, I asked them to turn I off.

I offered, "I think this man has abused his daughter sexually. I can tell by the way he preaches with so much exaggeration. I think he put his daughter in the hospital because if she's diagnosed as psychotic no one will believe her if she speaks about the incest."

There was total silence in the room. Then one of the residents stood up: "We have to apologize to you. We knew that this man had raped his daughter. He also had sex with her older sister by whom he has a child."

I responded, "Okay, from now on you are all going to respect me. Now let's talk about how to help this girl."

They had thought they were going to trick me into saying what a great father this man was and then reveal what he had done. From that day on, I had total respect from the residents. Actually, they were a little afraid of me and some of them said I was a witch because of what I could guess about people.

I assured them that I wasn't a witch—that there was no magic—that I just studied a lot. I also emphasized that I don't take anything for granted and that I think clearly.

In fact, I had not done any therapy while I was at the Mental Research Institute. I was working only on research. I had not totally transitioned from a psychoanalytic point of view to an interactional view that focuses on real relationships and not on what's going on inside people's heads. But by the time I was back in Buenos Aires, I had made that transition and I was reading all I could find on family therapy. There wasn't much. I read Virginia Satir, Salvador Minuchin, and Milton Erickson.

Virginia Satir was one of the founders of the Mental Research Institute. With a grant from the National Institute of Mental Health, in 1962 she became the training director of the first formal family therapy training program ever offered. She published the book, *Conjoint Family Therapy,* in 1964. She was interested in the relationship issues underlying the problems that people presented to therapy and she believed that improving people's self-esteem was essential to the success of therapy. When I came to the MRI in 1965, she had already left.

Salvador Minuchin was a psychiatrist, born and raised in the province of Entre Rios in Argentina. During Perón's first presidency, he was arrested as a political dissident and jailed incommunicado. When he was released, he enlisted in the Israeli Army during the 1948 war for independence. When I met him years later, he told me that my grandfather, Leiser, had given him boots for the soldiers in Israel. He was very grateful for that. He came to live in New York in the 1950s and published the book, *Families of the Slums*, in 1967, coauthored with Braulio Montalvo, a Puerto Rican psychologist. His method of family therapy consisted of disrupting dysfunctional relationships, causing the family to reorganize into more functional patterns.

In the 1960s, the only publication I had about the work of Milton Erickson—who later became the most prominent American psychiatrist—was a book edited by Jay Haley, titled *Advanced Techniques of Hypnosis and Therapy: Selected Papers of Milton H. Erickson, MD*. Most of the papers were very technical about hypnosis, but there were a few involving family therapy using indirect and paradoxical techniques. I was very interested in this approach. At this point, I had already made the switch from psychoanalysis to an interactional view, which was the aspect of Erickson's work that interested me the most.

Each time I took on a case at the hospital, I would make a decision about which of these three styles I would imitate. I recorded every one of my sessions, listened to the recordings carefully to critique myself, and then I would make a plan for the next session. I was very dedicated and thorough. I had no one to talk to about my work because nobody was doing family therapy in Argentina in those days. By imitating these different styles, I was eventually able to develop a style and a method of my own.

*   *   *

In 1970, the University of Buenos Aires organized a big international conference on family therapy. Among the invited speakers was Jay Haley, whom I had initially refused to meet. But by now I had made a drastic shift in my thinking about psychotherapy, and I wished I had taken the opportunity to learn from him. I was delighted when I was asked to be his interpreter at the conference.

Three days before the conference was to begin, I got a desperate call from the organizer. "Jay Haley is already here," he said. "He's in the hotel, doesn't speak a word of Spanish, and nobody in the team has time to entertain him. Please take him out to dinner tonight and spend the next three days showing him around the city, even if you can just do it for a few hours each day."

I felt I couldn't say no, but I had a bad feeling about this. I called Alberto on the phone and said, "This professor has arrived, and I'm being asked to take him out to dinner tonight. Please come with me. I don't want to be alone with him. You know how these American professor types are. I want him to see that I'm married, and I want him to meet you."

He refused, saying he had an important meeting. I pleaded with him, but he insisted that his meeting couldn't be canceled, and he chided me about being able to take him to dinner on my own.

I called my father, for whom Alberto worked, and asked him to tell him he had to accompany me. My father said he couldn't do that.

I picked up Jay from his hotel and took him to a fancy dinner in the colorful artistic neighborhood of San Telmo. The restaurant was in a colonial mansion and the waiters were dressed in 19th century attire. Jay ate the biggest steak I have ever seen. The dish is called "baby beef," and it's prepared mainly for tourists. Jay was respectful, no innuendos of any kind. We talked about communication theory and the book he was writing. He asked me many questions about the conference and the university. I thought I had been completely wrong about him. We agreed that the next day I would show him some of my favorite spots in Buenos Aires.

I spent the next three days, two or three hours a day, showing him what I like most or what I found most interesting about Buenos Aires. I couldn't spend more time with him because I was still nursing my baby. One day I took him to the first MacDonald's that had just opened in the city. He said he wished the hamburgers tasted like that at MacDonald's in the United States.

On the last day before the conference, I took him for English tea at a place called Queen Elizabeth. Argentina had been invaded twice by the British so there is a heavy British influence in the culture. Queen Elizabeth is a tea house in the center of an upscale shopping area in the city. It's elegantly furnished British style with comfortable leather chairs and dark wood paneling. Center stage is a portrait of Queen Elizabeth II, wearing a white dress with small roses embroidered on the side, a red satin cape, and a diamond crown. On the other walls are five or six fox hunting paintings with beautiful horses, dogs, the women sitting side saddle and everyone wearing black riding hats.

As on the previous days, we talked about therapy, systems theory, and the work of Milton Erickson. In the middle of the conversation, suddenly I was in a different place—a dark unpleasant room where I was sitting on a bed. I don't know if this lasted seconds or minutes. But suddenly, curtains were drawn, bright sunlight hit my eyes, and I was back sitting at the tea house. The experience was shocking, and I realized I had been in a hypnotic trance. He had hypnotized me without my consent. I pulled myself together, stood up, and said, "I have to go now. You can take a taxi." The next day the conference started, and I did a great job of translating his keynote address.

I never talked to Jay or to anyone about the hypnotic trance incident at the tea house. It was clearly an act of undue influence perpetrated on me against my will. He had hypnotized me without asking my permission to do so. Also, the experience was frightening and unpleasant. I wanted to deny it and pretend it had not happened. The experience caused me to never want to use hypnosis in my work. I can teach hypnotic strategies, but I only use hypnosis myself when helping children with nightmares or to control pain.

Jay liked Buenos Aires so much that a few months later he came back on vacation with his wife and one of his children.

CHAPTER 9

Death

By 1971, it became clear that we had to get out of Argentina. The dictatorship was cracking down on too many innocent people. There were paramilitary groups that were specifically targeting psychologists and economists. I was a psychologist and Alberto an economist. People in those fields were considered communists. Group psychotherapy was banned because it was thought to be subversive. We began to plan our escape.

My father said, "You're right to want to leave. This country is no longer a viable place to live. You will be the first to go to live in the United States and then the rest of the family will follow. All of us have to get out of here."

Alberto began to look for a job. A friend, who had been with us in the Ford Foundation Fellowship program, recommended him for a project at the Interamerican Development Bank. The project was in the Dominican Republic, and we spent a month there.

In those days, the Dominican Republic was like the Wild West. At the hotel or at a restaurant one could see that some of the men were carrying guns inside their jackets. I spent most of the time with my children at the beach. Often, young black boys would approach us and offer to dive for shells for the girls. When security came to tell the boys to go away, I would say, "These are my guests and they're having lunch with us here at the beach. Please call the waiter so we can order." And we all had lunch together.

Alberto did well with his project and was hired to work at the Interamerican Bank in Washington, DC. This suited me well because it would be 90 minutes by train to Philadelphia, and at the time the Philadelphia Child Guidance Clinic was the most prestigious place in the United States to work or to train as a family therapist. The director was Salvador Minuchin. Jay Haley was now working there and so was Braulio Montalvo, who had been working with Minuchin for a long time. I was hoping to be able to commute and work or get training there.

We arrived in Washington in December of 1971 and rented a house in Bethesda, Maryland, half an hour from downtown Washington DC and from the train station. I called Jay and asked for advice on how to find my way into the Philadelphia Child Guidance Clinic. He said there was a very interesting opportunity. They were starting a new project with grant money from the National Institute of Mental Health to train nonprofessional people from the community—mainly African Americans and Puerto Ricans—in family therapy. It was a two-year program, and at the end, the success rate of the non-professionals in doing therapy would be compared to that of professional therapists. They needed someone to teach family therapy in Spanish to the Puerto Rican students and to supervise them with the Spanish-speaking families they would work with. I was very qualified to do this. I made an appointment to meet with Minuchin.

I walked into Minuchin's office and said hello to him in Spanish.

He said, "We're going to speak in English because we are in the United States."

It was as if you met a fellow American in Russia, and the American declared, "We're going to speak in Russian here." It was just weird.

He then said, "Tell me about your life."

I said, "I'm going to sit down first if you don't mind." I was still standing. He had not offered me a seat.

I sat down in front of his desk and spoke directly, "I'm going to tell you about my professional life, not about my personal life."

As the interview continued, he was very aggressive in the way he asked questions about my training and career. At the end he told me I was hired for three days a week, but that I could only talk with the Puerto Rican students. He said I was too "upper-class Argentinian" to interact with the African Americans, and that I wouldn't "understand" them.

I agreed to this condition, but as soon as I started working, I forged some great relationships with the African American students and had great times with them.

At the end of the interview, Minuchin said, "I know this was a stressful interview, but this is a very stressful place and I had to see whether you could tolerate stress."

Actually, I wasn't stressed, I just thought that he didn't have any manners—that his mother didn't teach him good manners.

Soon after I started to work at the clinic, I was also training the psychiatric residents and the psychology interns. The program to train the lay therapists was a huge success, and at the end, we demonstrated that they were as good or better than the professional therapists. Yet nothing happened after that. The National Institute of Mental Health did not promote any similar programs.

It was a tiring commute to Philadelphia, because it took me two and a half hours to get there and two and a half hours to return. I wanted to spend the night at home because the children were young. What Minuchin agreed to pay me was so little that it barely paid for the commute, but it was worth it for me. That's how I gathered the case studies for my first book, *Strategic Family Therapy*. When we talked about how much he was going to pay me, Minuchin said, "You have a husband, and you have a wealthy father. I'm going to pay you barely the minimum. Why should I pay you more?" Obviously, today he wouldn't have gotten away with treating a professional woman this way.

To my surprise, months later, the psychiatric residents went on strike and marched around Minuchin's office with signs that said: "PAY CLOÉ WHAT SHE DESERVES." But he didn't. I think he resented that they did this, but I got a kick out of it.

One of the first things that Minuchin did when he became director of the Philadelphia Child Guidance Clinic was to transform every therapy room into a room with a one-way mirror and an observation room behind the mirror. The one-way mirror was the greatest invention that ever happened in psychotherapy. Until the introduction of one-way mirrors, psychotherapy was a secret relationship. The therapeutic conversation happened behind closed doors. Therapists' supervisors had to rely on what the therapist reported. These reports could be quite distorted and different from what the supervisor could directly witness. Now, with the one-way mirror, therapy could come out of the closet and actually be observed. The therapist was now accountable for what had transpired in a session, and the supervisor, when observing, was also accountable for the supervision. Add to this the phone or the intercom and the supervisor was not only observing but actually participating by giving instructions to the therapist.

I spent almost all my time behind the one-way mirror with a group of students, while one of them was on the other side of the mirror interviewing a family. I called the therapist with instructions over an intercom, or the therapist came out of the therapy room to talk with me. At any point, anyone on the staff could come behind the mirror and observe, so we were constantly under scrutiny. Often, Minuchin would come into the observation room and ask what I was doing. Every day was exciting and interesting, not only because of the families we helped, but because of so much interaction between students and teachers. We worked with very difficult disadvantaged families, and it was very fulfilling to help them to improve their lives.

Years later, there was much talk about how Minuchin had discriminated against women on the staff and treated them badly during those years. None of that was true. The truth is that he treated both women and men badly. He was blunt, harsh, and often ill-tempered, but it was not just with women. In spite of this, everyone loved him because he had transformed the clinic into the best therapy place in the country and because he really cared about the families we served.

One evening, late on a Friday, I was supervising a social worker from the observation room. She was working with a very disturbed adolescent girl who was cutting herself. The girl's parents were divorced, and the father had not seen the girl for quite some time, even though legally he had visitation. Present in the room were the girl, the mother, and a stepfather who was closer in age to the girl than to the mother. They were all very attractive, and I noticed there was some sexual tension between the girl and the stepfather. I thought that this girl was cutting herself because she wanted to be considered crazy so there would be no danger that she would become intimately involved with the stepfather. It's not uncommon for adolescent girls to engage in self-destructive behavior as a way of distancing and protecting themselves from a sexual encounter.

I called the therapist out of the room and explained, "What this girl is doing is very dangerous, but I don't want to put her in the hospital. What we have to do is find the biological father, get him to behave like a father and claim his rights, and she will feel protected. The cutting will stop. But if we put her in the hospital, she's going to be traumatized by that whole experience. I'm going to look for a psychiatrist who can take responsibility to keep her out of the hospital for the weekend." I couldn't do this because I didn't live in Philadelphia and I'm not a psychiatrist.

I couldn't find anyone in the building. Finally, I found the chief psychiatric resident who told me to put her in the hospital. It was Friday night, and he didn't want to be on-call all weekend. Furthermore, he said, she should be in the hospital anyway."

I said I wouldn't do that, and I continued to look for someone. I found that Minuchin was giving a seminar in a room with about 30 psychiatric residents.

I interrupted: "Excuse me Doctor Minuchin, I'm sorry to interrupt but you always say that patients come first here. I'm working with a family with a girl who has been cutting herself. I want to prevent her hospitalization, so I need a psychiatrist to back me up on this and I need to ask you to do it."

He told me to ask the chief psychiatric resident. I explained that I already had and was refused.

Minuchin stood up and excused himself. He walked down the hallway, found the resident, grabbed him by the jacket and yelled at him: "Don't you know what we stand for here? How can you not be supportive of Cloé?" And he has some other angry words. Then he went into the therapy room, talked briefly with the family, and then said that he wanted to speak alone with the girl.

He asked her, "What do you cut yourself with?"

"A razor blade," she said.

"Do you pick a clean one or a used one?" he asked.

"A clean one. I could get an infection with a used one." It was clear that her intent wasn't to commit suicide.

"Why do you do this," he asked.

"I hear voices that tell me to hurt myself. They tell me that I'm bad."

"Do you ever hear voices that say good things?"

"No, they just say bad things."

"It would be very nice," he said, "if they turned into good voices that say good things. I myself can hear entire symphonies in my head and I love it. I developed this talent when I was a political prisoner incommunicado in Argentina. I entertained myself listening to symphonies in my head. You should practice hearing good things."

He left the room and told me he would take responsibility for keeping the girl at home over the weekend. The therapist went back into the room and the girl said, "That doctor is crazy. I don't want to hear any voices—good or bad."

We found the father and asked him to use his visitation rights, take care of his daughter, be the father that she needed, and show the stepfather that he was the father. The girl needed him to take his place in order to feel protected. He understood, acted on this right away, and the girl was fine. She never engaged in self-destructive behaviors again.

There was a great team spirit at the Philadelphia Child Guidance Clinic, and I made many good friends there, including Braulio Montalvo. Minuchin, Montalvo, and Jay Haley were a trio of best friends who spent a great deal of time together and had interesting discussions. Jay had an ideal situation. Minuchin had recruited him from the Mental Research Institute with the promise that he could do as much or as little as he wanted at the clinic. Jay spent most of his time writing his book, *Uncommon Therapy*, about Milton Erickson, and he supervised the lay therapists we were training. Sometimes, he also talked with the residents and the staff.

*　　*　　*

My father died on June 3, 1973, in a car accident at the age of 56. He was driving with a friend to the golf club. A woman passed him on the highway, hit his car, and the car turned over. His seat belt wasn't fastened, and he died immediately. His friend came out of the car without a scratch. My sister called to tell me.

We flew to Buenos Aires that night. From the moment I told Alberto, through the trip and until we arrived at the funeral, Alberto was strangely withdrawn. I had already been talking to him about divorce, and I thought it was his resentment that caused his aloofness. Later, he told me that he thought I was lying, and that it was actually his father who had died. That, to me, was a crazy, shocking idea. Why would I lie about something like that?

I was devastated by my father's death. My mother had gone into denial and insisted that the coffin be opened so she could see that it was really him, which is against the Jewish religion.

The house was full of people, many of whom I had never met. There were many attractive women, who I couldn't help but think had had affairs with my father.

Days went by and my mother couldn't stop crying. Then one day, the wife of the Indian ambassador came to visit. She said to my mother, "You have to stop crying. When you cry like this you're hanging on to his soul and he can't go to where he has to go. It's bad for him." My mother stopped crying, and I never saw her cry for my father again.

After my father's death, several people came to see me and said that my father had been supporting their families and would I continue to do so. A psychiatrist, who had been the director of psychiatry at a hospital where I volunteered as a student, told me that my father had been giving anonymous scholarships, through him, to medical students.

I just reread several letters that my father sent to me in the months before he died. They were always addressed: "To my dear children and grandchildren" or "To Cloé, Alberto, Ingrid, and Magali," as if my young children could read or understand what he said. These were long handwritten letters explaining Argentine politics, but mainly trying to make arrangements to send me money and begging me to answer. Apparently, I never answered, and his letters became more and more despondent. I don't know what was going through my head that I didn't answer. Maybe I didn't want to tell him that I was on the verge of divorce. Maybe I was so self-centered and concerned about my own life that I just didn't pay attention to him. It's very sad for me to read the letters now.

In one of the letters, my father talks about the family therapy that my brother, sister, mother, and he were involved in. My brother, Claudio, had been acting crazy. He broke things, screamed, and talked nonsense. I knew that he was pretending to be crazy because he wanted to extort money from my father to make a film about life in the shanty towns around Buenos Aires. He had started the film and needed more money to finish it. I knew that Claudio had read Jay Haley's paper, "The Art of Being Schizophrenic," where he describes, in a humorous way and in detail, what you have to say and do for people to think that you're crazy. My sister had insisted on going to family therapy, which unfortunately consisted of my sister and brother attacking and blaming my father for whatever difficulties they were experiencing in their lives.

Maybe I didn't write to my father because I was ashamed—ashamed for having married Alberto—ashamed of having had children with him—and ashamed of wanting to divorce him. It's possible that if my father had lived, I would not have married Jay, who was much closer in age to my father than to me.

CHAPTER 10

Milton Erickson

Being in the midst of a painful divorce when my father died, I was overcome with grief. Jay Haley suggested that I see Dr. Erickson.

I called Mrs. Erickson and explained that I was referred by Jay and that I needed therapy to overcome my grief. She said that she would speak to her husband and get back to me. When she called back, she said that Dr. Erickson wanted me to come to Phoenix (where they lived) for a week. I explained that I had two little girls and couldn't leave them for so long, and she told me to bring them.

I flew to Phoenix and settled with my two daughters and the nanny in a nice hotel with a swimming pool so they would have fun while I was meeting with Erickson. He saw me every day for a few hours in his small office, sitting behind a desk in his wheelchair. He had other patients he had to see, so I waited in the living room of his house while he talked with somebody else and then went back in his office to talk with him. Sometimes, while he was seeing other patients, I went to the kitchen and talked with Mrs. Erickson.

It was hard for me to imagine that this old man from the American Midwest could possibly understand what my father had been like, how much I loved him, what Buenos Aires was like, my marriage. But I had to try to connect. I told him that not only was I grieving for my father, but I was in the process of a painful divorce and working under a great deal of pressure at the Philadelphia clinic. I explained that my career as a psychologist and therapist was very important to me. I had lived in California for three years because my husband had a scholarship to get a PhD at the University of California at Berkeley. I had always wanted to study at the Tavistock Clinic in London to become a psychoanalyst. My husband had promised that after Berkeley we would go to London, but he never finished his PhD, and I could tell that London was never going to happen because he now had a job at the World Bank in Washington DC.

Then the conversation circled back to how much I loved and missed my father. Erickson said, "You never had a father." I was irate. How could he say this to me when I was there grieving? He added, "Actually, you never had a mother either." Soon I realized that this was a strategy to get me out of my depressed state quickly. I was so angry at him that I couldn't be sad.

I talked at length about my career, about Jay who was pressuring me for marriage, about my experience working at the Mental Research Institute with the people he knew quite well. At one point I said, "This must be difficult for you because I'm here talking about Jay and I'm sure it's difficult for you to decide what to say to me because, after all, Jay is your disciple. He's writing a book about you."

He said sincerely and very respectfully, "When I'm with a patient, I only have my patient's interest at heart. You're my patient, I don't care about anyone else. Also, you're my colleague and I respect you as a fellow therapist."

I asked, "What do you think about Jay?"

"He's a cold fish," he answered. That was unexpected. I couldn't quite understand what he meant.

"Do you think my relationship with Jay could work?"

"Well," he answered, "Jay is a leader and you're clearly a follower, so that should work."

I was furious. "Follower," I thought. "You don't understand the first thing about me. I'll show you." I didn't say anything but at that moment I decided that my career was going to be at least as brilliant as Jay's. It was much later that I realized how skillfully Erickson had planted that ambition in my mind.

When I sat in the living room, waiting while Erickson talked with another patient, he gave me a book that he said I had to read. It was the biography of Margaret Mead, the renowned anthropologist, the author of *Coming of Age in Samoa,* and the wife of Gregory Bateson.

"Why do I have to read this?" I asked him.

"One day you'll understand," he said. In fact, there are many parallels between my life after my sessions with Erickson and the life of Margaret Mead. She also had two husbands, but they were not very important to her. What was most important was her work, especially her teaching. Bateson had told Jay that he had decided to divorce her when she started giving seminars early in the morning at the breakfast table. My entire life has been about my work and later I realized that by having me read Mead's biography, Erickson was saying that it didn't really matter who I was married to, my work was what was important.

What was most interesting to me about the conversations with Erickson is that up to that point in my life I had been excruciatingly shy. I had what today would be called panic attacks and terrible social anxiety, although we didn't use those terms then. If I had to be in a room with more than three people, my heart would pound so hard that I thought that people could hear it, and my hands would be so cold they felt frozen. This was a terrible handicap as a psychology student, as a therapist, and as a teacher. But I was there to talk about my grief, so I didn't mention this problem to Erickson.

When I left, after that week, I began to accept invitations to speak to 30 people, 50 people, workshops for 100 people, all over the country. I never had that panic and anxiety again. Erickson helped me to overcome this handicap without my ever even talking to him about it.

I think I was the last patient that Erickson saw individually. After that, he had become so prominent and had so many referrals that he only saw people in groups. He has been criticized for not treating women respectfully, but I didn't experience any of that. On the contrary, his encouragement was huge. I don't think my career would have been the same without those sessions with Erickson.

When I went back to Philadelphia, I said to Jay, "What does a cold fish mean?" I really didn't understand the term.

"Why do you ask?" he wanted to know.

"Erickson said you were a cold fish."

Jay never went back to visit Erickson, although he wrote several more books about Erickson's work.

Years went by, and I never contacted Erickson again. I published my first two books, which were very successful. I was invited to be a speaker at the first Evolution of Psychotherapy conference in 1985. The conference was a dream come true for me. Never in my wildest imagination had I dreamt that I would be presenting at the same level as legendary therapists, such as Carl Rogers, Bruno Bettelheim, Virginia Satir, Salvador Minuchin, R. D. Laing, to name a few. At age 45, I felt I was at the height of my career. I was the youngest presenter, with the exception of Jeff Zeig, the organizer of the conference.

Erickson had already died. The conference started with a reception for the presenters. Mrs. Erickson was there. She was sitting on a couch, and I went over and sat next to her.

I introduced myself: "Mrs. Erickson, you probably don't remember me, but I was a patient of your husband years ago and sometimes he would send me to the kitchen to talk with you when he had to see another patient. I was there for a week."

"I remember you perfectly," she said. "I know who you are. You never called and you never wrote."

At that moment, I wanted to drop dead. I felt so badly. Then I remembered that Erickson used to say that patients like to have amnesia for how they were feeling when they went to therapy. Should they contact the therapist later, when they were over the problem, it would take them back to how badly they felt at that time, and it could bring back the grief, panic, or whatever the symptoms were at the time of the therapy. I thought that Erickson probably understood, but I still could have sent a thank you note. It stays with me.

CHAPTER 11

The Paramilitary

Soon after I came back from seeing Erickson, I told Alberto that I was proceeding with the divorce. He said, "You have to know that I can't see past you."

When I asked what that meant, he said, "The girls."

"Are you threatening that you won't see the girls?" I asked.

He didn't respond. I thought that this was typical of the spouse who doesn't want the divorce, that this was an empty threat. He loved the girls, of course he would always be there for them. But it was not just a threat. He was telling the truth.

I told my lawyer that I didn't want any child support because I could support the children and I wanted the divorce to be as easy and quick as possible. He said that the judge would frown on the idea that the father—an economist with a very good job at the World Bank—would not pay any support for his children. I agreed to a compromise, settling for the very minimum, which was $200 a month for each child. Alberto never paid once. He saw the girls rarely, and soon he moved to New York to work for the United Nations and saw them even less.

About a year later, my lawyer called me and asked if Alberto was paying what he was supposed to. I told him Alberto had never paid. The lawyer wanted to put him in jail and insisted on it. I just wanted him to see the girls more often.

I always say that you don't really know someone until you divorce them. I had been absolutely certain that Alberto would never behave in this way. I was wrong, but his behavior confirmed for me that I was right in divorcing him.

Alberto died tragically in 1990 at the age of 54 when his car was hit by teenage drunk drivers on the road from Punta del Este to Montevideo, Uruguay. His third wife, who was in the car with him, was not hurt. The three teenage boys in the other car died. At the time, Alberto was the representative in Uruguay for the United Nations Development Program(UNDP).

*　　*　　*

Perón returned from exile in 1973 and won the presidential election by a landslide with his third wife, Isabel, running as vice president. In 1974, Perón withdrew his support for the Montoneros terrorist group. This was shortly before his death that year. During the presidency of his wife—who took over after his death—the far-right paramilitary death squad, Argentine Anticommunist Alliance (AAA or Triple A) emerged.

I was divorced and living alone with my two daughters in Bethesda, Maryland. One night I had a dream that I was lying by a large body of very cold water. My father appeared in the dream and started shaking me saying, "Wake up, wake up. You have to save your brother's life. Get up! Save him!"

"It's not important, it was just a nightmare," I thought. About an hour later my mother called and said my brother, Claudio, had been threatened by the Triple A. She had begged him to leave the country with his wife and children, but he refused. She had shown the threatening letter to a friend in the military who had said it was authentic. The letter said something along the lines of: "You're a Jewish pig and you're going to die." My mother and

Claudio thought the threat was because of the film he had made about the shanty towns in Buenos Aires.

Claudio's two sons were already going to school with two bodyguards, so it was ridiculous that he wouldn't leave. He spoke English perfectly and he had the money to go anywhere. I told my mother that I would come up with a way to bring him to where I was living in a suburb of Washington, DC.

I called Jay, explained the situation, and told him that he had to help me to save my brother's life. I had come up with an idea. I knew that Claudio wanted to make films and he was not working on any at the time. I called him and said, "Claudio, you have to help me. Jay and I just received a grant from the National Institute of Drug Abuse to make a film on addiction and we don't have a clue how to do it. We've never made a film. We have great footage of the family therapy of a heroin addict, but we can't use it because of confidentiality reasons. We would need actors to replicate the family, and we have no experience with actors. Please come and help us make the film. But you have to come immediately because the money has to be used in three months."

Claudio came with his family and he and Jay made the film that was used for many years to train therapists and drug counselors. The film's title is *Heroin, My Baby!* I was a consultant on the film. The whole process was interesting and fun.

Many years later, I told Claudio the truth. He wouldn't believe me, and my mother lied and said she didn't know anything about it. I think that Claudio simply could not accept our generosity and the fact that we had saved his life. This is another example of the many times in my life that people did not respond well to my generosity. Yet I value my generosity for what it means to me and not for how people respond to it.

Claudio was charming, sophisticated, brilliant, and had a great sense of humor. But he was a dilettante. He studied economics, but never finished the degree. His film about the shanty towns was never shown. For a couple of years, he wrote a column on couples' relationships for the highest circulation newspaper in Argentina, *El Clarin*. He was going to turn that into a book, but he never did. And he couldn't get himself to leave Argentina. After *Heroin, My Baby!* was finished, he went back to Buenos Aires with his family and bought a ranch in the province of Entre Rios, where he thought the Triple A would not come after him. Over the years he visited me many times, but I could never convince him to stay.

My sister, Nidia, was the same. She was also a psychologist, spoke English and French fluently, traveled all over the world, visited me many times, but she couldn't leave Argentina. It's always been difficult for me to understand that some people are so attached to their social context, so set in their ways, that they will stay in a county ravaged by terror, where their lives and their children's lives are in danger, even when they have the means and every opportunity to go elsewhere.

Nidia hated Claudio ever since they were children and for her entire life. She thought he lied, cheated, and was heartless. I thought he wanted to be liked by her and I tried to get her to see another side of him, but to no avail.

On one of Claudio's visits, I was working on my book, *The Secret Meaning of Money*, and I was stuck. I had written about 100 pages and couldn't figure out how to write more. He said he would help me. Every morning he would wake me up at 6:00, knock on my door (by then I was married to Jay, and we had separate bedrooms), and announce, "Get up, the fish is rotting at the market. We have to go to work."

I would get up and we would talk for hours. He didn't write a word. He just talked about his ideas. We had discussions and I wrote. He helped me and the book was soon done and is quite funny, thanks to him and his great sense of humor.

Eventually, Claudio became so addicted to nicotine that he couldn't travel anymore. He was also addicted to cocaine and alcohol. On one of my trips to Buenos Aires, my mother fell and broke her clavicle. He was very uncaring and outright cruel to her, and he yelled at me while he was on cocaine. I told him I would never see him or talk to him again. I didn't until many years later when he was very sick and in chemotherapy. He survived two cancers and eventually died because he had pneumonia and refused to go to the hospital because of his addictions.

*   *   *

My parents were always very social, but they became even more so when Claudio, Nidia, and became adults. They had many interesting friends. My father also had many lovers. I think he believed he was God's gift to women. The women were mostly wives of friends, who were also friends with my mother. One, I remember in particular, was seven or eight years older than me. On one of my visits to Buenos Aires, he introduced her to me, and I guessed they were having an affair. She lived with an old man who supported her. When he died, she bought a beach house in Punta del Este, right next to my parents' house. She was good friends with my mother and the two of them even went on a trip to Europe together, without my father. They also came to visit me when I first moved to the Washington, DC area. Eventually, after my father died, my mother found out about their relationship. She was quite upset, especially because of the money my father had lavished on her. He had even paid for a huge swimming pool overlooking the ocean at her beach house.

Another woman, who I suspected was one of my father's lovers, was one of the wealthiest people in Argentina. After my father died, she and my mother became very close, and they traveled all over the world together. I was happy because she helped my mother to overcome the grief over my father's death.

I thought the most interesting friends were a couple. The wife was never involved with my father in any kind of affair, and she was quite a bit older. As a young woman in Europe, her parents had sold her to a sheik, somewhere in the Middle East, maybe Saudi Arabia. She lived in the harem and became the sheik's favorite. When he grew old and knew he would soon die, he said to her, "I don't want you to stay in the harem after my death because my wife and son will treat you badly. I'm going to arrange for you to leave now and start a life in Argentina where you will be safe." He gave her a large amount of jewelry and sent her to Buenos Aires where he had arranged an apartment for her.

When she arrived, she went to a bank and opened a safe deposit box where she kept the jewelry. A young handsome teller at the bank noticed that every few months she came to the bank and removed something from the safe deposit box. He suspected that she was very wealthy. She was more than 20 years older than he, but he thought, "I'm going to seduce her and marry her. After she dies, I will probably have 20 years more to live a comfortable life." They married and he grew to truly love her. They were a wonderful couple. She lived to 100, and by the time she died, he was already old, sick, and close to death himself.

After my father died, my mother visited me frequently and stayed at my house for a couple of months. One time, she attended a workshop Jay and I were giving in another state. The psychologist who organized the event was a priest. We were going to be paid a percentage for the number of people attending the conference. My mother sat in the back of the conference room and counted the attendees and then told the organizer that there were more people than he was reporting. I said, "Mother, he's a priest. Don't embarrass me." She replied simply, "He still has to be honest."

Once we were sitting in my family room and my mother asked, "What are you thinking? You look worried."

I explained, "I have a workshop coming up with 200 people, and I have new material to present. I'm not sure that they're going to like it."

"Did they pay already?" she asked.

"Yes," I said.

"If they don't like it, do you have to give them back their money?"

"No," I said.

"Then, what do you care?"

She was very funny in her reasoning, but there was value to that. I've often used that phrase in therapy when someone is worried and obsessing about something, I might inquire, "What do you care?" or "Why do you care?"

Once I was sitting with a notebook on my lap, and she asked, "Why do you look so preoccupied?"

I said, "I'm looking at my to-do list and it's depressing."

"Read it to me," she responded.

Upon hearing all the entries, she asked, "When do you expect to do all this?"

"This week," I said.

"You'll be lucky if you can get all this done in one year," she said. "You need to learn to put things in a more realistic time perspective."

She was so right. Every time I drive myself crazy trying to do too much, I remember her words and slow down. I've helped many patients and students to be more realistic about time.

My mother sometimes could be quite a character in her innocence. She and my father went to Paris and visited Cecilio, my father's cousin who was a theater director. He was friends with Maria Felix, a famous Mexican actress who owned a night club in Paris and was known to be a lesbian. The three went to the nightclub and Maria sent to my mother, at their table, a bunch of red roses. My mother said, "How nice! In France, women give roses to women?"

On another occasion they went to a nightclub where there were many older women dancing with young men. My mother said, "How sweet! In Paris mothers go out dancing with their sons!"

My mother played bridge and won trophies until she died at the age of 86. She played every possible card game, and she loved to play poker with Jay because she always beat him.

In 2001, under a democratic government in Argentina, bank accounts were almost completely frozen and withdrawals from

U.S. dollar-denominated accounts were forbidden. This measure was known as "El Corralito," and was in force for one year. My mother lost almost all her savings, as did most of the middle class in Argentina. Many people committed suicide.

I had a boyfriend in the fourth grade at the American Community School in Buenos Aires. We were so close that his parents took him out of the school after the fourth grade because they felt it was an inappropriate relationship for our age. Years later, when I came back from Berkeley, I walked into the hospital, where I volunteered and there he was, standing in the hallway. We recognized each other immediately and embraced warmly. He had become a psychiatrist and a psychoanalyst. He said, "Do you remember that I gave you my stone collection?" I remembered. I think that was the greatest gift of love that I ever received from a man. He committed suicide in 2001 because of El Corralito.

CHAPTER 12

With a Little Help from My Friends

When one door closes … I was working at the Philadelphia Child Guidance Clinic, and Sal Minuchin invited me to lunch. He didn't have the money to renew my contract. The project to train people from the community was over. Braulio Montalvo had already left the clinic and had moved to Santa Fe, New Mexico. I knew that was a blow to Sal, because they had been working together for many years. I was sad to leave, but in a way, I was relieved because the commute was getting to be too much for me, and I wanted to spend more time with my children, especially after the divorce.

Jay was upset when I told him, and he soon told Sal that he would also be leaving. We began to talk about opening a family therapy institute in Washington, DC, near where I lived. Moving away from the Washington area was not an option for me, because the move from Argentina had been so traumatic and I didn't want to move the children again.

I was living in a suburb of DC, and I started applying for jobs as a supervisor and teacher of family therapy. I couldn't find anything. I called Sal to tell him I couldn't find a job and to ask for any words of wisdom.

He asked, "How many jobs have you applied for?"

"Three," I said.

"That's nothing," he said. "You have to apply to at least 18 jobs."

"Why?"

"Because 18 is the Kabbalah number for life. It brings you luck."

I said I would do that. But by the time I had written three more applications, I had three part-time jobs and several speaking engagements. I taught family therapy and supervised psychiatric residents, psychology interns, and social work students at Children's Hospital and at Howard University Hospital in Washington, DC, and at University of Maryland Hospital in Baltimore, Maryland, which was an hour's commute by car.

I was lucky in that the National Institute of Mental Health had just decided that they wanted the mental health professionals to be trained in family therapy and there were not that many qualified people in my area to do that. The work was very interesting and exciting, but hard. Working part time, I was expected to make every minute count. It was intense, but I had a one-way mirror at every hospital, and I loved the students. I didn't interact much with the rest of the teachers, who taught individual therapy and play therapy, because we disagreed on almost everything.

I told my students that when they were with me, they would be wearing one hat, but when they were with the other teachers, they had to make sure they were wearing another hat. I explained, "Family therapy works. And our therapies will be successful, but don't go around bragging about our successes or you will antagonize the rest of the staff." I've always been very protective of my students and very careful about not making enemies.

Actually, at Children's Hospital and at Howard University Hospital, the other professors never interfered with my work. But at University of Maryland Hospital, it was frequently a problem. I would get so upset by the carelessness and shortsightedness of my colleagues towards patients, particularly with children, that I would go straight to the director of training and tell him that I was quitting. It got to the point that he could tell just by the way I walked down the hallways that I was going to say that I was leaving. He would say, "Please Cloé, don't tell me that you're quitting. Just tell me what you want me to do, and I'll get it done."

One of the events that stands out in my memory was when they hospitalized a 5-year-old boy because he had temper tantrums. There were no beds in the children's ward, so they put him in the adolescent ward with severely disturbed teenagers. I wrote about this case in my first book, *Strategic Family Therapy*. I had him immediately discharged to his mother. It turned out that when he had a tantrum, he was pretending to be the Incredible Hulk, a character in a popular children's show at the time.

At University of Maryland Hospital, I was asked to do a research project, financed by the National Institute for Drug Abuse, on the family relationships of heroin addicts. I designed an instrument for measuring closeness and distance in family relationships and was able to show that heroin addicts had very strong family ties. The results were published in the journal, *Archives of General Psychiatry*, with the title "Family Ties of Heroin Addicts." Before this paper, addiction was considered a sociological problem. From that point on, it has been considered a psychological problem.

In 1974, Jay moved in with me and we opened the Family Therapy Institute of Washington, DC. We started out in an office space that we rented across the street from the National Zoo. However, I continued to work at the three hospitals. Jay insisted we get married, and finally convinced me, saying that it was embarrassing for him to be living with me outside of wedlock. When Sal found out that we were married, he threw a big wedding party for us in Philadelphia.

*　　*　　*

Operation Condor was a United States-backed campaign of political repression and state terror involving intelligence operations and assassination of opponents, officially and formally implemented in November 1975, by the right-wing dictatorships of the Southern Cone of South America. The United States government provided planning, coordinating, training in torture, and technical support, as well as supplying military aid to the Juntas. This support spanned the Johnson, Nixon, Ford, Carter, and Reagan administrations. Such support was frequently routed through the CIA. The program was intended to eradicate communist or Soviet influence and to suppress opposition movements against the participating governments. It was in existence until 1985.

It is not known how many deaths are directly attributable to Operation Condor. Some estimates are 60,000 dead, with roughly 30,000 in Argentina. Victims included dissidents and leftists, union and peasant leaders, priests and nuns, students and teachers, intellectuals, and suspected guerrillas. The so-called guerrillas were just scapegoats. They were never substantial enough to control territory, gain material support by any foreign power, or otherwise threaten national security. Key members of Condor were the governments of Argentina, Chile, Uruguay, Paraguay, Bolivia, and Brazil. Ecuador and Peru joined later.

Among the many prominent victims was former Chilean ambassador to the United States, Orlando Letelier, and his 26-year-old colleague, Ronni Moffitt, assassinated by a car bomb in downtown Washington, DC, not too far from where I lived. He was a friend of Alberto's.

Many of my friends, relatives, teachers, and acquaintances were imprisoned, tortured, or killed. Among them was one of my aunts, who was detained at the airport by the military when she was waiting to board an airplane to Brazil, in April 1977. The assumption was that she knew where the terrorist group Montoneros kept their money. I don't know whether she was tortured. At the time, her husband was in Canada. He was able to obtain her release at considerable financial cost.

Blanca Tarnopolsky was a professor of educational psychology at the University of Buenos Aires, and I took her class. One night, the paramilitary came to her apartment and took her, her husband, and two of their children. They then proceeded to the grandmother's house and took their 15-year-old daughter. They were never heard from again. One son in the family survived because he had been staying at a friend's house.

The son of my professor of Projective Techniques was tortured and killed. During this time, delinquency flourished, as is common when a society is in chaos. My aunt, Rebecca Madanes, with whom I was quite close, was kidnapped and held for ransom. I heard it on the radio in the car one evening when I was coming home from work in Washington. I was distraught and I couldn't communicate with anyone in the family. No one would answer the phone because they were waiting for the ransom call. The ransom was paid. One of the gang of kidnappers was her former chauffeur. After the ransom was paid, he was supposed to kill her and throw her body in the river. But he couldn't get himself to do that. He made her promise not to report him in exchange for which he'd allow her to live. He left her somewhere on a highway. Years later he was arrested, and she was asked to identify him, she said she didn't recognize him.

A 16-year-old girl—second cousin to me—had a boyfriend who was involved in some guerrilla organization. She went out with him on her birthday and never came home. Years later, the parents found out that the boyfriend had asked her to hold a briefcase for a minute. In the briefcase was a bomb that malfunctioned and exploded. She was killed.

Jacobo Timerman was an Argentine journalist who exposed the Argentine military's "dirty war," by writing an account of his incarceration in the late 1970s. He was a friend of my father's, and I met him once when he came to visit. Timerman launched a daily tabloid newspaper called *La Opinion*, which was very successful because of its attacks on abuses of power in high places. He was abducted by the military in April 1977 and was confined, tortured, and interrogated for two and a half years. After his release, he wrote a book, *Prisoner Without a Name, Cell Without a Number* (1981), which alerted the international community to the horrors taking place in Argentina.

Carlos Sluzki was the psychiatrist I had taken my last exam in Buenos Aires with when we both talked about coming to the Mental Research Institute. He finally came with his wife, Marilyn, in 1972. They, along with another couple, organized the Bay Area Latin American Refugee Committee in 1976. Marilyn coordinated the organization for several years, activating the "right to opt," which allowed many political prisoners from Argentina and Chile to obtain asylum in the United States. This included coordination with Amnesty International, an organization that seeks to protect the rights of political prisoners. The committee also coordinated with a couple of progressive Protestant religious organizations that offered the necessary sponsorship to activate the "right to opt," making the process even more legitimate.

Marilyn coordinated until 1982, and after that, she continued working on immigration for Latin Americans. I had a great deal of admiration for her because her work mostly consisted of recording the horrible, heart-wrenching testimonials of people who had been tortured. And she did this for years. Also, she often travelled to Buenos Aires for weeks at a time, where she lived and worked with Jesuit priests in trying to free political prisoners.

One time I was in Buenos Aires visiting my mother, at the same time that Marilyn was in town working with the priests. I suggested we have dinner together and include some old friends. She warned me that the CIA followed her everywhere and that I might get into trouble. I said I didn't care. We went to a restaurant with some other friends. Among them was Pepe Nun, who had been an important student political activist.

When I came back to the States, I was stopped and questioned at the airport by an officer I assumed was CIA. He knew where we had dinner, who was present, and what we talked about. He wanted information on Pepe Nun and on a professor of child development, Telma Recca, who had been my teacher and was considered a communist.

For 13 years, since my father died in 1973 until around 1986, I lived with constant anxiety about what could happen to my family and friends in Argentina.

*   *   *

Jay and I opened the Family Therapy Institute of Washington, DC in 1975 with the purpose of training family therapists in a strategic approach. By strategic, we meant that the therapist would make a plan for how to help a family and that the main tool of the therapist would be the directive—that is, the therapist would direct the family to interact in certain ways in and out of the therapy room. Furthermore, we would not use psychiatric diagnoses, and the focus would be on solving the problem that the family presented to therapy. The training consisted of lectures and live supervision of students doing therapy with the use of a one-way mirror. All the sessions were filmed. All the students were professional therapists, who wanted to learn about working with families.

We had a great group of students and working with them was fun. Eventually, we moved to a small house in Chevy Chase, Maryland, and then to a bigger house in Rockville, Maryland. Through my contacts at the University of Maryland Hospital, we obtained a contract to train all the therapists in the state. Maryland is a small state with around 2,000 therapists. This contract lasted for a couple of years. Some therapists were trained intensely with the use of the one-way mirror; others were in small groups; and some were in larger groups. We had a huge positive influence on how psychotherapy was done in the state.

Once I was working with the family of a very disturbed young man, who had been diagnosed schizophrenic. He had attacked his aunt, believing that she was having an affair with his father, and he had stabbed the family dog with a pencil. I had a group of students observing behind the mirror. At one point in the session, the young man got up from his seat and started pacing around the room behind me. I said, "Stop that and sit down. You're scaring me shitless." He sat down and began to talk normally. The students loved that. They had never heard of a therapist saying anything like that.

At the same time that we were growing the institute, we were building a house in Bethesda, Maryland, using some money that I had inherited from my father. The house was beautiful, but it took a great deal of time and work. Jay was giving workshops around the country, and he was typically paid a fee. I convinced him that we should organize his workshops as part of the business of the Family Therapy Institute. He wanted me to give the workshops with him because it would alleviate some of the stress of dealing with a group for a couple of days by himself. But I was very clear that I wanted to make a contribution first, and deserved to be teaching, and not do it because I was married to him. I had to wait until I was successful on my own. Also, I was still quite young. I didn't consider myself an equal. I didn't start giving workshops with Jay until my first book was published and was very successful. Until then, I was basically the secretary. I checked people into Jay's conferences and did all the administrative work.

Once, I organized a workshop for Jay in New York City. I was standing in a hallway with him during a break when a beautiful, elegant, dressed to the hilt, Annie Hall style, young woman came up to him and said, "Mr. Haley, I like you." I turned around and left. After a few minutes Jay found me. He was furious.

"Why did you leave like that?" He asked.

"You were with this beautiful woman," I said, "and I thought you might have an opportunity there. I didn't want to interfere." I was being truthful. Freedom is one of my most important values and I would never demand that a man be faithful to me if he didn't want to be. By the same token, I would never let a man control me in that way.

"Never do that again," he said. "You have to protect me from the crazies, not leave me alone with them. Don't ever do that again."

From then on, I protected him, and there were plenty of women who approached him.

*   *   *

When my first book, *Strategic Family Therapy,* came out in 1981, I was ecstatic. It was rejected by two publishers before it was accepted by Jossey-Bass. To this day, it is a textbook at many universities. Writing it was hard, but I felt the final product was good. I had succeeded in explaining how I think about therapy, and I had described many novel strategies. I believed that I had made a contribution to the field. When the reviews of the book began to come out, I was shocked by how Jay was constantly mentioned. So, I wrote this short tongue-in-cheek piece that was published in the magazine, *The Family Therapy Networker* (now, *Psychotherapy Networker*), entitled "With a Little Help from My Friends."

When I was a young girl my father said to me, "A woman needs to love a man she admires. You are too intelligent. I fear you will never find a man superior to you and you will never know happiness." My mother said, "You talk like a school-teacher, always lecturing. How are you going to find a man who can out-talk you?" Years went by and I wondered whether I would ever find a man that I could love.

Then I met Jay Haley. He was older, wiser, admired by everyone who I respected. We married and I was happy. Working with him, however, was difficult and sometimes humiliating. Students would say, "I want to be supervised by Jay." I was second best. Swallowing my pride, I thought, "One day I'll show them." Jay was helpful, understanding, and he taught me everything he knew. With his encouragement I began to write.

My first book was published and with it came repercussions in our marriage. I was brighter than either he or I expected. I had my own ideas, my work was accepted and admired. Students began to say, "I want to be supervised by Cloe." The balance of power in our marriage was disrupted. Jay became preoccupied. I remembered my father's words.

Little did I know that I had friends who would help me. The reviews of my book began to come out. First there was Howard Liddle in the American Association of Marriage and Family Therapy Journal. He reviewed my book and one of Jay's books in the same article. He said that just like Lucas and Spielberg had gotten together to produce the wonderful film "Raiders of the Lost Ark." Jay and I had come together to produce this wonderful work. I was puzzled. He was talking about two separate books, on different subjects, published in different years and by different publishers. I thought it was unfair that my book was not reviewed separately. One of our students said, "This is an example of male chauvinism. You are not considered a separate person from Jay." I was upset. Jay reassured and comforted me. I did not yet understand that Liddle's review was the first sign that our friends were coming to our rescue.

The book was then reviewed by Frank Pittman in the journal, "Family Process." Pittman said the book was good, but he devoted a whole paragraph to explaining how Jay is more charming than me. This confused me. Although Pittman knew Jay, he had never met me. How did he know that Jay was more charming? Also, I thought naively, "How is the issue of Jay's charm related to my book?" I showed the review to Jay, and he laughed. "Some of us are more charming than others," he said. With a twinkle in his eye, he added that he thought I was very charming. I thought that perhaps I should appreciate Pittman instead of taking offense.

Around this time, I read my good friend Minuchin's new book. To my surprise, I found that in one of the last chapters he talks about Haley and Madanes' technique of pretending. How could this be? Sal knew that I alone had developed that method. In fact, in his introduction to my book, he said, "Madanes' techniques of pretending are masterful and unique." How had they suddenly become the techniques of Haley and Madanes? "Sal is a great family therapist," I thought, "and I know he cares about me and Jay. I also know he likes to be helpful, and he often works in devious ways." Then I thought about Pittman and Liddle. "Perhaps," I said to myself, "there is more here than meets the eye."

That summer we went to Rome. We were giving a workshop for 200 people. I approached the room with some trepidation. Standing near the door was Maurizio Andolfi, who greeted me warmly in Italian. "The review of your book has just come out in my journal," he said. "I personally put it in Jay's hands." Back in the hotel, I read the review. It started, "This book was written by the wife of the boss." The wife of the boss! I was shocked. I told Jay. He asked, "How do you say 'boss' in Italian?" "Capo," I said. "Aha! Like in the mafia," said Jay, stroking his mustache. We had a wonderful romantic vacation in Italy that summer.

Back in Washington I began to work on a second book. I had new ideas. Students wanted to learn from me. Jay was becoming preoccupied. Then a new review of my book came out. It was published in the journal, "Social Work." by Gerda Schulman. She said that I do a good job of explaining Jay's idea of hierarchical incongruity. Jay's idea! That was one of the best ideas I ever had. In his introduction to my book Jay points out the importance of my concept of hierarchical incongruity as it relates to a theory of communication. But now I understood. I had met Gerda at one of my workshops in New York where she told me how much she enjoyed my work. I could see she was a kindly woman and a good therapist. She also was trying to help us.

Now I have finally appreciated our good friends—family therapists and writers—who love us and want to save our marriage. When things are not well between us, I take out the reviews of my book and go over them with Jay once more. The hierarchy is restored. Our good friends keep me in my place.

I must admit that some reviewers have taken a curiously different approach. The magazine "Family Therapy Networker," for example, published two reviews of my book. There is not a hint about Jay in either one of them. The journal, "Contemporary Psychology" and "The Library Journal," reviewed the book positively and did not even mention my husband. Of course, those reviewers were not interested in our well-being; they had never met us.

CHAPTER 13

The Generals

I met Virginia Satir at a conference at which Jay was presenting. I was a bit in awe of her because she was a pioneer and star in the world of therapy and beyond. She spoke to thousands of people and acted as a mediator in conflicts all over the world. She had been part of the Mental Research Institute before I was there. They knew each other well.

I said, "Virginia, my name is Cloé Madanes. I married Jay Haley."

She took my hand in her two hands in a comforting gesture, "I know. I'm sorry dear."

They didn't like each other. I believe that Jay didn't like Virginia's educational approach. She believed that therapists need to educate people about parenting and relationships. Jay had a more indirect approach, using metaphors and giving directives. I actually believe that there is room for both approaches. Sometimes education is sufficient and sometimes people need more. Virginia was all about love and self-esteem. Jay was all about power and hierarchy. He could be arrogant and dismissive.

In one of my books, *Sex, Love, and Violence*, I wrote about the stages of emotional and spiritual development in families. I proposed that at the lower level is the need to dominate and control one's environment—that is the need for power. At a higher level of spiritual development is the need to be loved. At an even higher level is the need to give love, to take care of others, and love them. At the highest level is the need to repent and to forgive. We all have done things that we regret, and we all need to forgive others for what they have done to us. Even though power is not only the power to dominate, but also the power to protect, I believe that power over others is the lowest form of relationship. Most therapists recognize the universal need to be loved, but I think I was the first to recognize the need to give love to others and the need to repent and to forgive.

After my first book was successful, Jay and I began to give workshops together all over the country and all over the world. They were typically two-day workshops. He would take the morning of the first day and the afternoon of the second day, and I would take the afternoon of the first day and the morning of the second day. We never presented jointly for fear of getting into disagreements in front of the audience. I felt that I had a gentler approach than Jay, and I was more interested in personal development and not just solving the presenting problem.

One time, we were giving a workshop in Calgary, Canada, and the Canadian psychologist who had organized the event, forgot to obtain the special work permit that is required for any foreigner who works there, even if it's just for one day. He told us about this permit two days before the conference, when it was too late to obtain it. Two hundred people had already registered. We were bringing professional looking videotapes with us, and we were concerned about being questioned at the border. The organizer suggested that if we were stopped at customs, we should say that we are visiting friends and plan to discuss our videos with them.

The problem was that Jay could never lie when it came to his professional life. He flew into Calgary a couple of hours before me. When I arrived, the customs officer saw my videotapes and asked me what they were for. I said that I was visiting friends and was going to discuss the videos with them. He said, "You're lying. Your husband has already been detained. He told us that you're both giving a workshop and you don't have the work permit. We are putting you on the next flight back to Washington, DC."

"Fine, I said. "I will go back. But you need to know that tomorrow you will have 200 Canadian citizens here at customs wanting their money back. They already paid and the money is in my bank account in Washington. I'm not giving it back. Maybe your government wants to give them the money."

He understood. "All right, I will let you both in. But don't do this again."

*   *   *

Our work was an intrinsic part of our marriage and we constantly talked about our students and about the family therapies we were supervising, as well as what to teach in our workshops. We discussed and critiqued the work of other teachers. Jay was always writing a book. Soon I realized that if I talked about some idea that I had over dinner, the next morning I would find that he had already written it up and it was sitting by his typewriter. When I confronted him with this, he would say, "Ideas are in the air. They don't belong to anyone in particular."

I would counter by saying that they belong to the person who have them in the first place. "I have to publish and take care of my career. You can't take my ideas and publish them," I insisted.

Soon I refused to talk about anything that interested me for fear that I would find it written up in his next book. When he wrote his book, *Leaving Home*, I read every word of the manuscript and took out every sentence that I thought belonged to me. All this was not good for the marriage, but it was good for me in the sense that it forced me to write. Not only did I fear that Jay would steal my work and publish it before I had a chance to write it myself, but because we taught thousands of students all over the world, I feared that if I didn't publish my ideas, some student would.

Yet we had many good friends and many good times. I took frequent vacations of at least two weeks with the girls, and also sometimes with friends. I'm not a good swimmer, but my passion is swimming and snorkeling in warm, calm, transparent waters. And I have a great deal of endurance, so I can stay in the water for hours. We went several times to the French and Italian Rivieras and cruised the Greek Islands. We visited practically every island in the Caribbean and every island in Hawaii.

*   *   *

Simja was a second cousin to my father by way of his father, Leiser. He was a young man at the beginning of the war in Poland and he was recruited into the Russian army, in spite of being Jewish. After terrible hardship, he was one of only two survivors in his battalion. He made his way to Israel, where he became a terrorist fighting against the British alongside Menachem Begin, who became his good friend. When I met Simja in Buenos Aires, I was impressed by his character and strength. He told wonderful stories about the war and the early days of Israel.

When I married Jay, we went together to Israel and visited Simja at his home. He showed us pictures of the family members murdered by the Nazis. His greatest pain was that when he was taken away, his younger sister was 16 years old, and he never found out what happened to her. He assumed the Nazis had killed her.

We took a trip to Israel as a vacation with my daughters soon after the invasion of Lebanon. We were staying at the King David Hotel in Jerusalem at the same time Kissinger was there. One day, Jay got a call from a psychologist with the military, who wanted to consult with him about a difficult situation. Jay said that he was on vacation with his family, but that the psychologist— who I will call Jonathan—could join us that evening for dinner at the hotel.

We sat down to dinner with the girls. Jonathan came and said he didn't want to have dinner. He just wanted a quick consultation with Jay. He explained that several generals in the Israeli military were suicidal because they had lost so many soldiers during that war, and they blamed themselves for making many mistakes. He asked Jay what could be done to prevent their suicide. Jay said something along the lines that this was a terrible situation, and he really didn't know what could be done.

I had been listening to this quietly, behaving like the wife of the respected professor, but I couldn't contain myself. "Excuse me but can I say something?" I piped up.

Jay responded, "Of course, go ahead."

I told Jonathan not to argue with them about their mistakes and their guilt. Say that yes, they made terrible mistakes and they lost so many soldiers. But now, there are all these widows and all these children who don't have a father. The generals must live to take care of them for the rest of their lives, so that those mothers and their children can have a life with all the protection and opportunities they would have had if the husbands and fathers had lived. Say that dying is easy, staying alive and fulfilling your responsibilities is hard.

Jonathan thanked me and said he would do this.

Years later, a group of Israeli therapists came to the institute for a training program. One day, I was teaching about suicide prevention, and I talked about this conversation with the military psychologist. They said they had heard about this in Israel. The psychologist had done exactly what I suggested and none of the generals had committed suicide. They were dedicated to taking care of the widows and the children of the soldiers.

I had many interesting experiences in Israel. One time I was giving a workshop by myself in Tel Aviv for about 200 people. I talked about my method for preventing the recurrence of sexual abuse and violence, which I covered in two of my books, *Sex, Love, and Violence,* and *The Violence of Men.* The approach consists of 15 steps that the therapist follows with a family. Some of the most important steps are to talk about the spiritual pain that is caused by the abuse and to have the offender kneel on the floor in front of the victim and express sorrow and repentance for what he did.

A man in the front of the room raised his hand and said that this was interesting but not applicable in Israel because Jews don't kneel in front of anyone, not even God. An Orthodox Jew, dressed in black with the curls and the hat, stood up in the back of the room and said angrily, "First of all, that man in the front is an ignoramus. Of course, Jews kneel in the temple on the day of atonement. And you," he said pointing to me, "you are a plagiarist because all this is in Maimonides."

"Maimo who?" I asked. "Can you give me that reference?"

In those days I had not heard of Maimonides. I looked him up when I got home. He was a philosopher in Spain who fled during the Inquisition and left his writing behind in his house. There was a mudslide, and his books, which had been preserved under the mud, were recently rediscovered and translated into English. They are important philosophical essays. I found that Maimonides does say that there is only one circumstance when a man should kneel in front of another human being, and that is when he has offended a woman sexually.

Recently, I met with Simja's son, who was in San Diego for a conference. We went out to lunch and talked about the family. I mentioned Simja's sister and the pain he carried all his life not knowing how she died.

He said that something incredible had happened just before his father's death. When he was very ill, the rabbi came to see him and said that it was a matter of hours until he would be gone. Then the mailman came and there was a letter from Berlin. He opened it and it was from a woman who said she was in a nursing home with Simja's sister, who was very old and didn't see well enough to write and had asked her to write it. She wanted to tell Simja that she had survived because she married a German soldier and lived all her life in Berlin. She had been ashamed about marrying a German and that was why she never contacted the family.

Simja died a few hours later knowing that his sister had lived.

*   *   *

General Videla's military dictatorship in Argentina was succeeded in 1981 by General Viola, who, with the Dirty War near its end, could not control the military. He was pushed out by General Leopoldo Galtieri, who was determined to fulfill Argentina's historical claims to the Falkland Islands (Islas Malvinas) by armed force. Argentine troops landed in the Falklands in April 1982. A British naval force sailed to the islands, and on June 14, 1982, the Argentine military governor surrendered.

Galtieri resigned and general elections were announced. Raul Alfonsin, a civilian lawyer, won the election for the Radical Civil Union on October 30, 1983. The military government and hundreds of military personnel were prosecuted for human rights violations. British Prime Minister, Margaret Thatcher, won a landslide victory for her Conservative party in the parliamentary election of 1983.

The Falklands campaign could not have been mounted, let alone won, without America's help under President Ronald Reagan. The United States repositioned a spy satellite and supplied 12.5 million gallons of aviation fuel, along with hundreds of missiles and other military equipment. The Thatcher-Reagan relationship altered history and caused great economic woes for the United Kingdom.

Reagan was diagnosed with Alzheimer's disease in 1994, but he was probably undergoing a gradual mental decline that was visible during the 1984 presidential debates. Alzheimer's disease can take as long as 20 years to develop. It's possible that Thatcher was also suffering a mental decline while she was still in office, because soon after she was diagnosed with dementia. Two world leaders with declining faculties and a deranged military dictator who thought that he could take on Britain, caused an unnecessary war in which thousands of men were killed.

It was after the Falkland War that I decided to become an American citizen. I found that even after the war was over, it was difficult for me to travel to some of my favorite places, like London and the British Virgin Islands, with an Argentine passport. I told Jay that the girls and I would finally become American, and after a ridiculously long and tedious process, we became American citizens.

*　　*　　*

Jay never learned to pronounce my name. He called me Cloi. My name is Cloé, which in Spanish, French, or English can never be pronounced as Cloi. I didn't care, but Alberto said to me, "How could you have married a man who can't even pronounce your name!" I just ignored this issue.

Another challenge was his sister. Jay had a brother, I met briefly. He was retired and dedicated to painting landscapes of Jackson Hole, Wyoming. He was a nice man, and his paintings were lovely. Jay had a sister who was a big, tall, blonde, crass, fun woman who made anti-Semitic remarks in the presence of me and my children. This was the sister whom Jay loved. He especially enjoyed going with her to gamble in Las Vegas. She was a heavy smoker, like Jay had been, and she eventually died of lung cancer. The other sister, Jean, was a successful administrator high up in the California government bureaucracy. I am forever grateful to her because she helped me through a difficult time with Jay. He listened to her and respected her. Jay was the youngest of four and he used to say that he and I got along in spite of the age difference, because I was the oldest of three and he was the youngest of four.

I had challenges with Jay, not only in protecting my authorship and intellectual property, but also in managing our institute. When we moved the institute to a small house in Chevy Chase,

Maryland, we hired an administrative assistant. She was a nice young woman, about 10 years younger than me. Soon I realized that she had some kind of infatuation with me that made me uncomfortable. She was incompetent in her work, and she followed me around constantly. I had my own private bathroom, as part of my office, on the second floor of the building. She was the receptionist who was supposed to be always on the ground floor by the entrance. I would go to the bathroom in my office suite, and when I came out, I would find that she was standing by the door, as if she had been trying to listen to what I was doing in the bathroom.

I told Jay that we had to give her a good compensation and fire her, but he wouldn't let me do it. Fortunately, his sister Jean came to visit. One day we were sitting on the deck of our house having a drink, looking out on the beautiful garden, and I said, "Jean, please help me. You manage thousands of employees and I have a problem with one assistant that I think we need to fire, but Jay disagrees." I told her about the situation. She told Jay to fire her, and he did. Later we discovered that she had made many serious mistakes that we were not aware of.

Some years later, when we moved to a bigger office building in Rockville, Maryland, my sister came to visit. She too was a psychologist and she was interested in observing my work. After one day at our institute, she said to me, "Why do you have an office manager who hates you?"

I said, "Oh, you noticed?"

She said, "Of course, everyone can see that. You have to fire her."

"It's not easy," I said. "I don't know what reason to give so I won't have legal problems."

She advised me to say that I appreciated her work and the fact that she was so intelligent and competent, and that she was overqualified for the job and she should go back to school and get a PhD in psychology. The final touch—that I'd write a letter of recommendation so she could get into graduate school.

I did exactly that and she left happily.

When I arranged for a vacation on the Big Island of Hawaii, Jay said he would prefer to go to Las Vegas to gamble with his sister. We went to Hawaii, and he was so unpleasant that I decided to cut the vacation short so he could meet his sister in Las Vegas.

One day, after shoveling snow on the driveway of our house, Jay told me he was having chest pains. Our doctor examined him and said the symptoms were beyond his expertise and Jay should go to the Mayo Clinic immediately to get a diagnosis. I went with him, and they told us that because Jay had been a chain smoker, his arteries were blocked and in some strange way, his capillaries had replaced the arteries. They knew of only one similar case. They couldn't predict if he would live, or for how long.

We went back home and decided to go on with our lives. But Jay became more and more withdrawn and began to show the signs of Parkinson's disease. I noticed that something was wrong, but didn't know what. Jay was very stoic and didn't like to complain about pain. As a child, he had undergone a hip operation that was botched, leaving him with a limp and with considerable chronic pain. Sometimes he was in a bad mood, which I often took personally, only to realize later that he had been in pain. I asked him many times to tell me when he was in pain, so I would know his behavior wasn't about me, but he wouldn't do it.

Throughout my life with Jay, I kept trying to get Alberto to see the girls more frequently. I gave him the key to our house and told him that whenever he was in town he could stay in the house. He did that from time to time, and he even threw parties there a couple of times. Jay was very tolerant of this, except for when we would come home from a trip and find that Alberto had drunk the bottle of Scotch whiskey and not replaced it. Jay would go from the garage straight to the liquor cabinet and announce, "Alberto was here. The whiskey is gone."

When I eventually divorced Jay, Alberto came to see me. He said, "Now that we're both divorced and we are both older, the sexual part of the relationship is not so important. Let's get married again." I said no. If he had been a better father, I might have remarried him, but as it was, I had no respect for him.

CHAPTER 14

R. D. Laing

By 1970, R. D. (Ronnie) Laing was very popular as part of the anti-psychiatry movement. Thousands of people attended his lectures. His books, *The Divided Self, The Self and Others, The Politics of the Family*, and *The Politics of Experience*, had a profound intellectual impact. Jean Paul Sartre wrote the foreword to the book Laing coauthored with David Cooper, *Reason and Violence: A Decade of Sartre's Philosophy*. Laing had opened and eventually closed Kingsley Hall, an alternative treatment facility for severely disturbed patients, who were allowed to experience their psychosis without medications, restrictions, or coercion. He had lived in India for several years. He had experimented with LSD, and he drank heavily. I admired him and felt a deep connection with him through his books, even though I knew that he was prone to shock audiences with his antics, which I had not witnessed, yet but had heard about.

One day, I heard that R. D. Laing was coming to Washington to give a workshop on rebirthing. The topic didn't interest me, but I couldn't miss the chance to see Laing in person. Rebirthing is a therapy technique that was somewhat popular in the 1970s.

The idea is that people suffering from anxiety, depression, and other symptoms, have not been able to overcome the trauma of their birth. Even though nobody can consciously remember passing through the birth canal, the memory lies deep in the unconscious. By reliving the experience with a psychotherapist in a group, the person can be freed of the anxiety that originated at birth.

I told Jay that I was going to Laing's workshop, and I wanted to invite him to lunch at our house on Sunday after the workshop was over. Jay knew Laing well and liked him.

He agreed that would be nice and interesting. We often invited prominent therapists who were passing through Washington.

The workshop was not good. Ronnie and his wife, Jutta, were on stage wearing jogging outfits. They invited people in the audience, who were interested in the experience of rebirthing, to come onstage. One by one, they took a person, embraced them tightly and asked the rest of the group to participate, jumping one on top of the other, with the original participant almost suffocating, crouched on the floor. Many of them cried when they were finally let go, and this was considered a release of emotions, after reliving the traumatic birth experience.

Fortunately, the workshop was for only one day. At the end, I went up to Laing, introduced myself as Jay Haley's wife, and invited him and his wife for lunch the next day at our home in the garden. He accepted the invitation.

It was my housekeeper/cook's day off, so I enlisted my oldest daughter and a friend of hers to help me cook and serve. We set a beautiful table under tall trees. It was a two-course meal and dessert, with plenty of wine. The dessert was my specialty, chocolate mousse made the real way with raw eggs.

Ronnie and Jay had a very interesting conversation about therapy. I asked Ronnie if he was planning to write another book like *The Politics of the Family* and *The Politics of Experience*, two of my all-time favorites in the field of mental health. He said that it was a good question and that he was now writing poetry.

At the end of the meal, he asked for cognac, which I provided, and he drank quite a bit. Later my younger daughter told me that by accident she opened the door of the guest bathroom, and he was vomiting. He had a reputation for drinking excessively, but I thought he seemed sick.

During that long lunch we became good friends and promised to see each other again in the near future.

About a year later, we heard that Ronnie was going to be in New York, and we planned to meet him at the bar of The Plaza for lunch. My sister came from Argentina because she wanted to meet him. The conversation with Ronnie, as usual, was very interesting. Jay said, "Ronnie, you always have your finger on what's happening that's important in the world. What would you say is going on now?"

"The power of social work," said Ronnie. "It's much worse than the power of psychiatry and it's going to become even worse. In Europe, social workers are taking children away from their parents without due legal process."

Both Jay and I found this hard to believe.

But Ronnie told us he had personal knowledge of the trend. He said he had a friend in Denmark whose 12-year-old son was taken away because she had empty bottle of wine in the garbage. He said, "You'll see. When it starts happening here in the U.S. it will be even worse."

Of course, he was right. In a matter of months, social workers were taking children away from their parents without due process and at our Family Therapy Institute we were desperately trying to help those parents to recover their children.

At one point during the lunch, my sister stood up. "I'm going to the bathroom. Come with me," she demanded.

I was puzzled but I followed her. Her message for me: "I can tell you're attracted to him. You have a happy marriage and he's a drunk. You're just attracted to him because he's identical to our father. Don't be stupid. Stay away from him."

Ronnie truly looked identical to our father. They could have been twins, or certainly brothers. He even stuttered when he was excited and so did my father. We went back to the table.

I had brought chewable vitamins B and C and I kept giving them to Ronnie. He took them but wondered why I was giving them to him.

I explained that the vitamins counter the effect of the alcohol, so he wouldn't get drunk.

"I will get drunk anyway," he said. "I'll just have to drink more, and it will be more expensive."

The next time we met was in London. We were there because we had given a workshop in Cambridge. Ronnie invited us to the theater and then to his house. There were two other guests—a couple of young people—he introduced to us as some kind of German terrorists. We drank, smoked some pot, which in those days was illegal, and Ronnie played the piano beautifully for us.

I asked Ronnie if he saw patients in the house.

When he said yes, I pressed further. "In this room? Or do you have a study?"

"I'll show you where I see patients," he said. "It's in the garden."

He grabbed my hand and pulled me to the garden with Jay following behind us. He was grabbing me very hard trying to embrace me. Jay had to pull him away. I think he might have hit him.

Shortly after, we went back to the Claridge where we were staying. Jay said, "Ronnie is so brilliant. It's too bad that he gets drunk and makes a fool of himself."

The next time I saw Ronnie was at the Evolution of Psychotherapy Conference in Phoenix, Arizona in 1985, sponsored by the Milton H. Erickson Foundation, with 5,000 therapists attending. The presenters were the therapists who had made the most important contributions to the field. Among them were Carl Rogers, Bruno Bettelheim, Salvador Minuchin, Virginia Satir, Carl Whitaker, R. D. Laing, Jay, and me. It was an extraordinary event.

Later I learned that Ronnie arrived from London without a bag or a change of clothes. Jeff Zeig, the organizer of the conference, took him to buy a jacket and a change of clothes. Ronnie wanted to find a patient for a clinical demonstration. He wanted someone who had been diagnosed psychotic but was not on medication. With the help of some social workers, Jeff found a young homeless woman, who refused medications. The young woman, Christy, agreed to be interviewed at the conference. A small room was set up behind the stage, with a cameraman, and the interview was projected into the large conference room where thousands of therapists were seated.

Ronnie conducted an extraordinary interview with Christy, or perhaps, Christy conducted an extraordinary interview with Ronnie. The following is the exchange that was most remarkable. It was lost on the audience with only a few people understanding what went on.

Ronnie and Christy had been talking about spirituality for about five minutes. The issue was whether there is a universal mind, and if there is, can we understand it.

Christy abruptly changed the subject and said, "I asked him why he didn't kill himself and he said that he is not ready yet." She spoke in the third person—somewhat in the direction of the cameraman, as if she were talking about him—but she was really talking about Ronnie. She added, "I guess that if you are dead, then you blow any chance of doing anything good for anyone, huh?"

Ronnie said, "This time around, anyway." (Meaning "in this life" or "in this reincarnation.")

There was a long silence, and then Ronnie said, "If we were just sitting here without these cameras on, I wouldn't say anything just now, but I feel impelled to make an effort to keep talking for the sake of the people listening."

I knew that Ronnie had severe bouts of depression and that he had often contemplated suicide. In five minutes of conversation, Christy had realized this. She talked in the third person, but she was really talking about Ronnie. It was her way of telling him that she understood that he had suicidal thoughts. It was also her way of helping him by reminding him that he had a mission as a therapist. His mission was to help others and that's what kept him alive. She was being his therapist.

Ronnie understood this and he showed her he understood by saying that there's no need to continue talking. They had made a deep connection and didn't need to say anything more. By connecting with Christy at a deep spiritual level, he had managed to switch roles with her, and she became coherent and sane. He then invited her to come on stage with him where she talked to the audience, intelligent and composed, even though she had to witness Ronnie being attacked and criticized by people in the audience who didn't understand what he had just accomplished. The interview with Christy had been masterful and very moving. Jay, Sal Minuchin, and I understood this. I am not sure how many others did.

The next time I saw Ronnie was in Amsterdam in 1986. He invited me to give a paper at a conference he was organizing with the title, "Eros and Violence." I said that sounded rather pompous for a professional conference, and that while I could speak about violence and about family therapy, about eros I knew very little. A more matter-of-fact title like "An International Conference on Family Therapy" would be better, I suggested. He said that "Eros and Violence" represented the central human dilemma of our time, but that he would consider another title, since perhaps my view represented that of other speakers as well.

After this telephone conversation I thought about how I had admired Laing's work since my college years. I realized that at least I owed him the respect of giving some thought to the subject of eros and violence. I decided to try to figure out what he meant when he said this was humanity's basic dilemma. Ultimately, I wrote a paper about love and violence.

A couple of months before the conference, Ronnie called to confirm the details. He said he was sending the brochure with the new title, "An International Conference on Family Therapy." I said I had written a paper, with great effort, on love and violence—the crucial issue of our time—and that was what I was going to present. Later, I learned that the conference had been advertised not only as "Eros and Violence," but also as "Love and Violence," "Eros and Relationships," and "Violence and Family Therapy."

As it turned out, the conference took place a few days after the nuclear accident at Chernobyl and the radioactive cloud floating over Europe reminded us that the boundaries that separate life and destruction are as tenuous as those between love and violence. The paper I gave in Amsterdam became the main theme of my book, *Sex, Love, and Violence: Strategies for Transformation*. It was also published with the title, "The Goals of Therapy," in the *British Journal of Family Therapy*.

The conference was also memorable to me because I had the opportunity to meet the Dalai Lama XIV, Tenzin Gyatso, whose writings had a great influence on my work. The Dalai Lama was going to give a keynote address at the conference, but his speech was cancelled because there was a terrorist threat on his life. Instead, the main speakers were invited to visit the Dalai Lama at his home, in the outskirts of Amsterdam. We were a small group—Ronnie, Virginia Satir, Rollo May, Jay, and me. The house was heavily guarded by German soldiers with machine guns. We waited in a room for a few minutes before the Dalai Lama came in dressed in his orange tunic and sandals. We stood up and he came over to shake our hands one by one. When he took my hand, I looked into his eyes, and instead of pupils, there were flames—like the flame of a candle in each eye.

I don't hallucinate. When I see something, I know it's real. So, when we came out of the house, I excitedly said, "Did you see that—fire in his eyes? There was a candle in each eye!" They made fun of me and joked about me. No one had seen that. I have never experienced something like that again.

We sat down after the handshake and the Dalai Lama talked to us about how important our work as therapists is in current times. He said that people don't go to monks, priests, or rabbis anymore. They come to us. As therapists, we are in a very special leadership position because for so many people, we have replaced religion.

The next time I saw Ronnie was at a dinner party at Loren Mosher's house in Washington DC. Ronnie was a good friend of Loren, who was our psychiatrist at the Family Therapy Institute. Loren was a wonderful person, very kind and dedicated to treating patients with respect and to preventing the abuses of psychiatry. When Jay and I arrived at his house, we were invited to sit outside on the deck where dinner would be served. Loren was in the kitchen making champagne risotto. Ronnie was sitting at the table. I sat next to him, and Jay was across from me. Ronnie's wife, Margarita, was inside the house.

I had recently seen the play *Dangerous Relationships* on Broadway. It had been a big success both on Broadway and in London. I asked Ronnie if he had seen it and he had. We began an interesting conversation about the play. The theme—the possibility of driving someone crazy by creating an intense relationship and then destroying it—was of interest to me. Suddenly, Margarita, who must have been seven or eight months pregnant came out on the deck and started screaming at Ronnie, something along the lines of, "There you are, sitting with her— always with her. You only care about her!"

I stood up and said, "Margarita, please come and sit here. I'll move over there," pointing to the other side of the table.

Ronnie grabbed me, sat me roughly on his lap and said in my ear, "This is for you."

Jay pulled me away, again almost hitting Ronnie, and said that we were leaving.

As we walked to the car, Loren came out and was very apologetic. We reassured him we were not offended in any way. Ronnie is the way he is, and we were not upset.

I had my own interpretation of the situation. I knew that Ronnie was writing a book on jealousy. I think he had created a fabulation by which he convinced his wife that he was having an affair with me, just to make her jealous so he would have material for his book.

The saddest part for me was that when Ronnie died in St. Tropez in 1989, Loren came to the institute to tell me that Margarita had requested that I not attend the funeral. The service was held at Saint Paul's Cathedral in London and was attended by people from all over the world. Apparently, she still was thinking that I had an affair with Ronnie.

CHAPTER 15

Tony Robbins

The field of psychotherapy was in decline. It was the later 1980s. First came the pharmaceutical companies with their promises of quick cures, disregarding pernicious side effects, turning us into a nation of drug addicts, colluding with teachers and child psychiatrists to use medications for social control in the classroom and within the family. Then came managed care companies, demonstrating that everything good can be turned into its opposite. They took the concept of brief therapy and used it to prevent access to treatment and to downgrade the profession to the lowest level of pay, where in many cases, a therapist could make more money cleaning houses than doing psychotherapy.

Then came the marriage of managed care companies and pharmaceutical companies—a union that is truly demonic. Psychiatrists began to avoid the practice of psychotherapy and devoted themselves exclusively to the dispensation of medicine. Psychotherapy was no longer taught to psychiatric residents.

The old biological model of causation that Freud encountered at the beginning of his career, arguably now has as much prestige as it did 100 years ago. Why? Not because of the impeccable scientific research behind it. In fact, there is still no evidence that emotional problems and interpersonal difficulties are the result of brain disease. Medications, and the biological view of psychopathology that justifies their use, dominate the discussion again because they serve the interests of the two major players in the mental health world: the drug companies eager to expand their markets for psychotropic drugs, and managed care organizations equally eager to restrict or even eliminate talk therapy in favor of cheaper and faster chemical behavior modification.

Meanwhile the power of the departments of social services all over the nation has grown out of control. Thousands and thousands of children and adolescents have been taken out of their homes, allegedly for their own protection, placed in foster homes, usually going from one foster home to another, and getting further and further away from their communities. The least fortunate are placed in institutions far away from their families where they are warehoused for years, bringing enormous profits to the corporations that run these institutions and that collude with the social workers in denying the existence of relatives and refusing to help the immediate or the extended family so that children can go home.

While all this was happening in the United States, my work was getting more recognition in Europe. In 1996, I was invited to the University of Zurich to receive an award for my contribution to psychology, anthropology, and philosophy. Days before my trip, the news broke about the Swiss banks refusing to give money back to the surviving family members of Holocaust victims. On receiving the award in Zurich, I had to give a short speech. I said that it was my hope that Swiss citizens would pressure their bankers to return the money to the survivors of the victims of the Holocaust. There was total silence in the room, and afterwards I didn't get one comment on my speech, but it felt good to speak the truth. Switzerland wasn't neutral during the war. When there is a conflict between good and evil and you're neutral, it means that you're on the side of evil. I could feel that anti-Semitism was still very much alive among the Swiss people.

At the Family Therapy Institute, we had fewer and fewer students because therapists were not making enough money to be able to pay for specialized training in family therapy. Jay and I divorced, and he moved to California. I got an offer to work for one of the warehouse institutions in Virginia to train their therapists. Naively, I believed I would be able to train therapists and change their practices. I moved to Virginia and soon realized that they only wanted me there to show that they had a prestigious family therapist on their staff who was known for helping parents and for preventing the institutionalization of children. I stayed for six months and saved a few children, returning them to their families, but there were 700 children jailed in the institution. About a year after I left, the institution was closed because of rampant sexual abuse of the children.

*　　*　　*

In November of 2001, I was in Santa Barbara, California, visiting one of my daughters and her family. Because I was on vacation, I hadn't read my emails or picked up my phone messages for a few days. When I did, there were several urgent messages from the Tony Robbins' company. They were saying that Tony wanted to invite me to Fiji to a seminar he was giving. I had no idea who Tony Robbins was. I called back and said I would be happy to meet Mr. Robbins somewhere in the United States, but Fiji was too far away. They explained that Tony owns a resort in Fiji and that this seminar would be unique because it would be for only 50 people, whereas his regular seminars are for thousands of people. He wanted me to attend the five-day event and then discuss it with him. He thought I would be able to focus better on his presentation if there were fewer people in the room. They apologized for the tardiness of the invitation, but said I had to leave for Fiji in four days. They had forgotten to invite me earlier because of the upheaval in everyone's lives after the 9/11 attacks.

I really didn't want to go, but my son-in-law said that Tony was a very successful speaker and would be interesting. He encouraged me to go, saying it would be a vacation.

I went to a bookstore and found two books by Tony, but they were so long that I couldn't possibly read them before the flight. But I found one audio recording that was just two hours. I told my son-in-law that I'd purchased the tape and that it was two hours long—the exact time it would take to drive from Santa Barbara to the Los Angeles airport. I made it clear that if he said one stupid thing, I'd be turning around and coming back.

Not only did Tony not say one stupid thing, listening to that tape changed my life. I got on the plane and began to write furiously about all the changes I would make, everything that I would do differently—my goals, my mission, how I would recover my mission.

When I arrived in Fiji, Tony and I hit it off immediately. He is very funny and charming, and we discovered that we think alike about so many things. He had heard about me because a friend had given him one of my books, *Strategic Family Therapy*. He showed me the book and he had underlined almost every page.

Both Tony and I come from the Milton Erickson tradition, so we think alike, and we work alike. Tony studied with John Grinder, who was Erickson's disciple and one of the creators of NLP (Neuro Linguistic Programming). I studied Erickson's work, I was his patient, and I worked with Jay who was his disciple.

I told Tony that underlining everything in the book wasn't how you do it. "You only underline what's important, I said. "Everything is important in this book," he answered. Of course, right then he had won me over. No author can resist liking someone who praises her book.

On the evening before the seminar started, we had dinner with the coaches who would work in the seminar, assisting the participants and making sure that everyone was comfortable and understood the presentation. The main group of 50 participants would at times be divided into smaller groups working with a coach. At the dinner, I was sitting at the table with Tony on my right and an empty seat on my left. The coaches were told that during the dinner, if they had a question for me, they could come up and talk to me from that empty seat. A young man came to sit next to me. He said, "I have a question about a woman in my group. I never worked with someone like this before. Her name is Astrid. She is in her 30s and has her own very successful business. She was gang raped when she was 12 years old. She doesn't date, lives alone, has never had a boyfriend, has never even lived with a girlfriend. I think she hasn't overcome the trauma of the rape."

"You have to get on your knees in front of her and tell her that you want to apologize to her in the name of all the men in the world who would have wanted to protect a little girl and not hurt her."

"I can do that," he said. "Thank you."

I didn't realize that Tony was listening to our conversation. During the seminar, he asked Astrid to stand up and he gave the apology I had described in a way that brought tears to the eyes of many in the audience. I was very moved. Astrid said nothing and there was no expression on her face.

On the last day of the seminar everybody was walking on the beach, looking at the sunset, and Astrid came up to me. "Cloé, can I walk with you? I have something I want to tell you."

"Of course," I said.

"I did something I've never done before in my life," she said.

"What did you do?"

"I asked a man for a date, and he said yes." She smiled happily.

"That is so wonderful! You made my day," I said, and hugged her.

When someone has been deeply hurt, an apology is necessary. If it can't come from the perpetrator, it needs to come from someone else.

One evening, Tony and I were having dinner alone and he asked me, "What is your mission?" I talked about the institutionalization of children and teenagers, the absurd diagnoses that they're given, and how they're mistreated, drugged, and incarcerated.

He asked for an example.

I told him the story of a boy in the institution in Virginia where I had been working. The story was so sad that Tony began to cry. I stopped eating because I thought it was impolite to eat while he was crying. Then, his soon-to-be wife, Sage, came into the room and he asked me to tell her the story and she began to cry. Neither of us finished the dinner.

On another occasion, I told Tony that I would like to see the films of his interventions. During his seminars he asks for a show of hands of someone who is depressed, or suicidal, or has a relationship problem. He picks one person at random and begins a conversation to help the person to overcome whatever challenge he or she is experiencing. I had noticed that there was a professional crew filming the seminar.

"Some of your interventions are excellent," I said. "I would like to see the films."

"I don't have any films," he said. "We film for archives. The footage is saved in archives."

"Tony, I can take that footage and make great films that will be used to train many generations of therapists."

We discussed how the films could be made and we decided to partner. Eventually, the partnership became Robbins-Madanes Training. We have more than 100 films, and together with Mark and Magali Peysha, have trained 20,000 life coaches from all over the world. Many of our students are therapists who want to add coaching to their toolbox. Many are professionals in other fields, like medicine or law, and want to learn how to understand and connect better with their clients. Others just want to apply the concepts to their own family and to create a better life.

*　　*　　*

In 2002, I was invited by the state department to give a talk on terrorism to government officials and therapists in Panama. My talk was on how to establish leadership in a time of crisis. I decided to spend a few days in Panama instead of going back to the States right after the talk. Some people from the department of education heard that I was staying longer and asked me to give a workshop for educators.

It turned out that the day before my workshop a group of high school students had vandalized the school and there was much destruction. The educators were shocked, as this had never happened before. I heard about it at the beginning of my workshop and decided to set aside what I had prepared to present, and instead talk about how to prevent violence from happening again in schools.

I based my talk on Tony's concept of the six universal human needs:

1. Certainty—To feel secure, safe, to know what is going to happen next.
2. Uncertainty/Variety—To be entertained, to have some novelty and excitement.
3. Significance—To feel respected, important.
4. Love/Connection—To feel loved or at least connected with others.
5. Growth—To develop one's skills, to learn new things.
6. Contribution—To give to others.

The first four needs must be fulfilled for survival. But not everyone, particularly the poor, get to fulfill the needs for growth and contribution.

These needs are universal for everyone, but people fulfill them in different ways. For example, someone may fulfill the need for *certainty* by knowing where the next meal will come from. Someone else might need to have one million dollars in the bank to feel certainty. For *uncertainty/variety,* someone might want to watch television, whereas someone else might need to race cars. This type of spectrum exists for all six needs.

I discussed how, if children and adolescents were able to fulfill the six human needs at school, there would be no violence, no vandalism, no bullying. If teachers gave as much importance to making sure that each student fulfills the six needs in the classroom on a daily or weekly basis, as they give to the material they're teaching, there would be no reason for students to feel angry or resentful. To my surprise, a woman stood up and said, "I'm the secretary of education and this program will start to be implemented in all schools by tomorrow." I was happy and amazed.

The atmosphere in the country was very tense and fearful because it was expected, right after the September 11 attacks, that the next terrorist attack would be on the Panama Canal. I was welcomed to the country by the American ambassador and his wife who showed me around and were delightful. One day, we were going to drive to a restaurant with a chauffeur, and as we were getting in the car, I sat in the back on the right side, which is where I usually sit when I have a driver. The ambassador said, "I think it's better if you move to the other side because where you are is where I usually sit, and if there is an attempt on my life, they will kill you instead." I moved quickly. This was how intense the fear of violence was in Panama at the time.

In 2003, Tony was invited to Venezuela by the Carter Center at the height of political tensions when many international observers feared an outbreak of civil war. The Carter Center had been involved with Venezuelan politics since 1996. The purpose of the trip was to facilitate peaceful negotiations between the supporters and the opponents of President Hugo Chavez. William Ury, a professor in the school of negotiation at Harvard University, was also invited. Tony asked me to come with him because of my fluency in Spanish and my understanding of Latin cultures. We flew to Caracas together on a commercial airline—he and I and an ex-Marine, who was his bodyguard.

Caracas looked like a city on the verge of a civil war. There were few people or cars on the streets. The only hotel that was open was the Marriott and that's where we stayed. There were shortages of all kinds, and only one cafeteria style restaurant was open with a minimal menu. My room didn't have the usual amenities. The carpet and curtains were shabby.

The day after our arrival we were picked up by a car and driver and taken to the office of the Carter Center nearby where we were briefed about the situation in Venezuela and what the center was doing to try to bring about peaceful negotiations.

Later we had lunch with about eight politicians, all men. I sat next to Tony in order to translate for him. When we talked about this meeting afterwards, I realized that he had understood the dynamics and the power structure just by the men's tone of voice and body posture.

The bodyguard never left our side during our trip. Once he said to me, "I know that I make you uncomfortable, but please don't keep trying to get away from me. I have to stick to you at all times. It's my job."

We met with Bill Ury, who was very charming and soft spoken. He explained that in every political conflict there is a third side: the people who care more about peace than about who wins the conflict. Tony liked the idea and suggested that we could rent a space and hold an event for the people on the third side. We talked to the people at the Carter Center and planned the event for which they rented a large theater. Citizen leaders on both sides of the conflict were invited and the meeting was open to anyone who wished to attend.

Tony said to Ury, "You have very good ideas, but your delivery is not so good. You're too soft spoken and unemotional. When you speak at the event, people are not going to relate to what you're saying. Let me coach you so you can come across stronger."

It was fun to watch Tony coaching him. The two men couldn't have been more different from each other.

Almost a thousand people came to the event and the national guard was called out for fear violence might erupt between partisan groups. The atmosphere in the theater was tense and fearful. Both Tony and Ury spoke, mobilizing the group to be a force for peace. The day before there had been a confrontation in the streets between the factions that were for and against Chavez, but instead of fighting, they ended up playing soccer. This was a good sign.

Tony and Ury rallied the audience to express, with a great deal of screaming, that they wanted peace—that peace was more important than the opposing interests of the groups; that winning was not worth the suffering and death that a civil war would bring. At the end of the meeting, a committee was formed for the purpose of bringing peace to Venezuela.

There were soldiers with machine guns everywhere during the event. At the end, there was a room set up with drinks and appetizers, but we discovered that the soldiers had eaten mostly everything.

Chavez had agreed to an interview with Ury, but only with him. We had breakfast with Ury the day he was meeting with Chavez. I asked him what he was going to say, and he said he didn't know. He was going to play it by ear.

I asked if he'd like to hear a little about the history of Venezuela so that he'd know where Chavez was coming from.

I explained that during the war of independence from Spain, there were two important generals. One was San Martin in Argentina and the other was Bolivar in Venezuela. Bolivar wanted to unite all of South America into a United States of South America. San Martin opposed this and wanted Argentina and Chile to be separate independent countries. Unfortunately, Bolivar died young before he could fulfill his dream, and San Martin prevailed.

I explained that Chavez was a big admirer of Bolivar. I told him that if he talked to Chavez about what Bolivar would have done in this situation, he would listen. I said, "Tell him this is his opportunity to be like Bolivar."

I don't know what transpired in that meeting of Chavez with Ury, but he felt it was successful. We left Caracas thinking that there wouldn't be a civil war—and there wasn't.

Writing in the Time of Covid

I MIGHT NOT HAVE WRITTEN this memoir if it were not for the pandemic. I not only had the time, but I needed to do something very difficult that would take all my energy and would require intense focus and clarity of mind. I enjoyed it, and also suffered through it. Like Ernest Hemingway said, "Writing is easy. You just sit at the typewriter, and you bleed."

Any kind of writing takes courage because you expose yourself to criticism, misunderstandings, accusations, and humiliations. But writing about your life takes a special courage because you can't stop thinking about how you may come across as self-indulgent, self-aggrandizing, full of self-pity, or frivolous.

One thing that I learned while writing this memoir is that what I remember most are the small, marginal things that happened at the same time as the big events that shaped my life and over which I had no control. The dress I wore, the movie I saw, the book I read, a poem—these things are more vivid in my mind than the upheaval, the exile, the persecution, and the fear. It's as if I had two lives: one was about what was happening around me, what others did to me; and the other was my inner life, what truly mattered to me—the life that is unique and personal.

I have been very fortunate because my life always had meaning. I decided at a very young age that I wanted to devote myself to helping others, and that I wanted to make a contribution to psychology—and I did both. And I continue to do it. Never mind the upheavals, the conflicts, the grief, the failures—I never wavered for a moment about what gave meaning to my life. And I'm grateful for that.

In this memoir, I wanted to create a bridge between my social context and my personal life, as these influenced my thinking about therapy, what I chose to focus on, and the way I look at human dilemmas. I hope I have succeeded in making that bridge. In this sense, nothing that I did was by accident.

Tony Robbins says that everyone's life is either an example or a warning. Looking back, I think my life was both. I believe that, given the cards I was dealt, I did quite well for myself and for others. I leave it up to my readers to decide—an example or a warning?

REFERENCES

CHAPTER 1

De Beauvoir, Simone (1953). The Second Sex, Alfred A. Knopf, New York.

Deutsch, Sandra McGee (1986). The Argentine Right and the Jews 1919-1933. Journal of Latin American Studies, Vol. 18, No. 1 (May, 1986). Cambridge University Press

Freud, Sigmund (1917). Introduction To Psychoanalysis.

Potash, Robert A. (1980). The Army and Politics in Argentina, 1945-1962: Peron to Frondizi. Stanford University Press.

Sartre, Jean Paul (1938). Nausea. Editions Gallimard.

Sartre, Jean Paul (1944/1989). No Exit. Vintage; Reissue edition

Steinbeck, John (1952/2016). East of Eden. Penguin Classics

Stekel, Wilhelm (1943/2015) The Interpretation of Dreams: New Developments and Technique. Cole Press

CHAPTER 2

Caplan, Gerald (1964). Principles of Preventive Psychiatry. Tavistock Publications

De Ségur, Comtesse (1858). Sophie's Misfortunes. Hachette, Paris, France.

Kafka, Franz (1915/2019). The Metamorphosis. SDE Classics

Kafka, Franz (1919/2008) Letter to His Father Oneworld Classics (under the title Dearest Father).

Longfellow, Henry Wadsworth (1898). The Song of Hiawatha. Minnehaha Edition F.M. Lupton Publishing Company.

Neruda, Pablo (1924). Veinte Poemas de Amor y una Canción Desperada. Editorial Nascimiento, Santiago, Chile.

Robbins, Anthony (1991). Awaken the Giant Within. Simon & Schuster

CHAPTER 3

Crawley, Eduardo (1984). A House Divided: Argentina, 1880-1980. St. Martin's Press.

CHAPTER 5

Bowlby, John (1953). Child Care and the Growth of Love. Penguin Books, London

Klein, Melanie (2002). Love, Guilt, and Reparation: And Other Works 1921-1945 (Writings of Melanie Klein). Free Press

Laing, R. D. (1965, rev. ed.). The Divided Self. Penguin Books

Moreno, Jacob Levy (1947). The Theater of Spontaneity. (2011: Northwest Psychodrama Association)

CHAPTER 6

Faúndez, Julio. (1988). Marxism and Democracy in Chile: From 1932 To the Fall of Allende. Yale University Press

McPherson, Alan. (2016). A Short History of U.S. Interventions In Latin America and the Caribbean. Wiley-Blackwell

Salgari, Emilio (2013, Nico Lorenzutti, translated) The Black Corsair. ROH Press

CHAPTER 7

Rascovsky, Arnaldo (1995). Filicide: The Murder, Humiliation, Denigration and Desertion of Children by Parents. Jason Aronson Inc. Publishers

CHAPTER 10

Mead, Margaret (1928). Coming of Age in Samoa. William Morrow Paperbacks; Reprint edition (February 20, 2001)

CHAPTER 12

McSherry, J. Patrice (2012). Predatory States: Operation Condor and Covert War in Latin America. Rowman & Littlefield Publishers.

Pinter, Harold (2005). Art, Truth, and Politics: The 2005 Nobel Prize Lecture. Three Essays Collectives

CHAPTER 13

Middlebrook, Martin (1986). Operation Corporation: The Story of the Falklands War, 1982. Viking Adult

Behind the One-Way Mirror: Revised and Updated

After more than three decades, Behind the One-Way Mirror is as an essential resource now as ever. Why a revised edition? Because Cloé Madanes is a singular voice in strategic therapy, whose clarity and intellect can light the way for everyone working on the front lines of human relations — therapists and life coaches. Ms. Madanes has updated this important contribution to reflect an evolution in her own thinking: "I realized that now we possess a body of knowledge that can help millions of people and that we need to share this knowledge so that everyone can benefit from it, instead of limiting it to a small group of people who belong to the therapy professions." (2019). Zeig, Tucker & Theisen, Inc., Phoenix, AZ

Changing Relationships: Strategies for Therapists and Coaches

Caution: Don't be deceived, this little book packs a big punch! Changing Relationships is a deep repository of practical insight that will inspire dozens of aha! moments. But Madanes' observations are not simply impressive; she is also a wise and generous mentor, providing access to powerful strategies that can be put to immediate use by therapists and coaches. Madanes isn't much interested in "fixing" people, rather, her brilliance is in helping people to discover — or to recover — the pathways that will lead them to becoming what they want to be, both as individuals and in relationship. (2018). Zeig, Tucker & Theisen, Inc., Phoenix, AZ

Relationship Breakthrough

Everyone faces the challenges of making relationships work, whether with spouses, family members, friends, lovers, or colleagues. Relationships have the power to make one feel happy, frustrated, or miserable. In Relationship Breakthrough, Cloé Madanes – an expert in creating healing and empowering relationships – gives readers vital tools to transform their relationships and their lives. Madanes' cutting-edge methods produce real results and create rewarding, sustainable relationships. Using simple step-by-step exercises and drawing on the examples of clients who have benefited from these techniques, Relationship Breakthrough teaches readers how to resolve long-standing family conflicts, how to synchronize their needs with those of others, and how to create outstanding relationships in every area of their lives. This is the first book that ties the guiding principles of Tony Robbins' work with Cloé Madanes' revolutionary approach to relationship therapy. (2009). Rodale Books, Emmaus, PA

The Therapist as Humanist, Social Activist, And Systemic Thinker

Reflecting some 25 years of Madanes' thinking on essential aspects of theory and practice and her innovative approaches to working with those from whom others may back away, this collection will both inform and inspire. From the early years to the most recent pieces, Madanes is clear in her conviction that dramatic change for the better is possible and that therapists can foster such change, that free will and a system that follows its own rules exist simultaneously; and that the human spirit has the capacity to triumph in the face of all kinds of adversity. The Therapist as.... Provides an opportunity to see what such conviction looks like in action across a variety of circumstances. It also teaches us about the power of humor even in the most serious settings. And just as each piece captures something essential of the author at that particular time in her life, each piece also tells us something of the time itself as reflected in the voice of the author. (2006). Zeig, Tucker, & Theisen, Inc., Phoenix, AZ

The Violence of Men

Renowned family therapist Cloé Madanes presents a therapy of social action, a proven model of therapeutic intervention developed for professionals who work with violent men. At the very heart of this approach is the conviction that the offender is fully responsible for his actions. As evidence of this core belief, a therapy of social action requires the offender to acknowledge his violent actions, demonstrate authentic repentance, make amends to the victim, and find acceptable alternative behaviors. (1995) Jossey-Bass Publishers, San Francisco.

The Secret Meaning of Money

Internationally known psychologist Cloe Madanes and writer Claudio Madanes present a revolutionary view of the role money plays in families. In dozens of stories, anecdotes, and case histories, they show how family members use money in covert ways that express desires, struggles for power, and yearning for commitment. To prevent money issues from destroying relationships, the authors present extraordinary problem solving techniques that use money to restore and heal family relationships. (1994). Jossey-Bass Publishers, San Francisco

Sex, Love and Violence

This work proposes a model for choosing the right intervention to solve the problems brought to therapy. The emphasis is on how to understand and control the many forms of violence (including incest and sexual abuse) that constitute a primary therapeutic problem of our time. (1990). W. W. Norton & Co., New York

Strategic Family Therapy

A classic work which uses imaginative techniques to help achieve balance within the family. It gives attention to specific problems such as violence, drug abuse, and depression, and seeks the hidden meaning in these symptoms, which are clues to the underlying family structure. (1981). Jossey-Bass Publishers, San Francisco

ACKNOWLEDGMENTS

First and foremost, I want to express my appreciation to Suzi Tucker, the best editor in the English language. I am grateful to my daughter, Ingrid Sojit, who suggested that I write this memoir, who gave me the title, and whose unfailing criticism kept me on my toes. My old friend, Juan Floriani frequently nudged my memory. Grace Jackson carefully read and commented on the manuscript. I wish to thank my friends, Ken Keacher, Tonita McKone, Eleni Oikonomopoulou, Morgan Peterson, and Glenn Wood for their comments and encouragement. I am especially grateful to Jeff Zeig who has steadfastly cheered me on throughout the decades.

Cloé Madanes, HDL, LIC is a world-renowned innovator and teacher of family and strategic therapy and one of the originators of the strategic approach to family therapy. The author of numerous classics in the field — *Strategic Family Therapy; Behind the One-Way Mirror; Sex, Love and Violence; The Violence of Men; The Secret Meaning of Money; The Therapist as Humanist, Social Activist and Systemic Thinker; Relationship Breakthrough and Changing Relationships* — her work has been translated into 20 languages.

Ms Madanes has won many awards for her distinguished contributions to psychology and has been featured in Newsweek, the Washington Post, and the Boston Globe. She has keynoted for such professional organizations as the American Association of Marriage and Family Therapy, the National Association of Social Workers, the Evolution of Psychotherapy Conference, the Erickson Foundation, and the California Psychological Association, among others.

Cloé Madanes is President, Robbins-Madanes Training (rmtcenter.com).
cloemadanes.com; madanesinstitute.com